AF585157

Social practices, pedagogy and language use: studies in socialisation

Edited by

Peter Mickan, Ioana Petrescu and Judith Timoney

with EL Benn, Shannon Blackman, Kelly Brown, Adam Hamilton and Vanessa Raschella

Contributors

Ray Adams, Simon Eddy, Glenda Inverarity, Dongjin Kim, Mi-ok Lim, Peter Mickan, Johanna Motteram, Ioana Petrescu, Fiona Ryan and Judith Timoney

LYTHRUM PRESS
Adelaide

First published by
Lythrum Press
54 Currie Street
Adelaide
South Australia 5000

December 2006

ISBN-13 978-1-921013-13-3
ISBN-10 1-921013-13-3

Cover artwork by Megan Boyd, University of SA
Designed and typeset in Giovanni by Michael Deves
Printed and bound by Hyde Park Press

CONTENTS

Preface

The essays in this book have been written for teachers and education students. They are investigations into teaching, learning and language use in varied settings. The essays are based on work carried out in Applied Linguistics at the University of Adelaide. I have been privileged to work with postgraduate students in the Discipline of Linguistics over the last six years during which time we have studied the discourses of social practices. Students wrote the chapters that document their practical investigations written for studies in Applied Linguistics.

I have many people to thank. First and foremost my students whose scepticism and enthusiasm have continually challenged me. The teachers and school administrators with whom we have worked are an inspiration to me and to my students. I am very grateful to teachers for the opportunities to learn from observing their work and seeing their work represented in the studies and research conducted by my students.

In the South Australian Department of Education and Children's Services I have been fortunate to work with an outstanding team of professionals who support *English as a Second Language* (ESL) programs in schools. I single out for special mention the ESL program manager, Don Boereman and the ESL Policy and Program Officer, Rosie Antenucci, with whom I have had many intensive discussions helpful for working out ideas relevant to ESL pedagogy.

My co-editor Dr Ioana Petrescu from the University of South Australia, assistant editor Judith Timoney, and editing students under Ioana's guidance, EL Benn, Shannon Blackman, Kelly Brown, Adam Hamilton and Vanessa Raschella have been meticulous in their work and congenial to work with. At the University of Adelaide I have been encouraged by my colleagues. Research grants from the Faculty of Humanities and Social Sciences at the University have enabled my students and I to pursue questions informing the essays in this book.

Peter Mickan, Adelaide, 2006

Introduction

The purpose of this book is to examine learning as a social phenomenon situated in people's practices. The essays explore aspects of socialisation in different settings. Researchers and teachers wrestle with complex theories of learning, which at times seem unrelated to classroom experiences and unhelpful for planning instruction. When I've been invited to give presentations at workshops and conferences, I've been warned that teachers do not want too much theory. The links between theory and practice are seen as tenuous and theory as marginal to teaching.

Theories draw upon different and sometimes contradictory academic traditions—psychological, social and linguistic—which often appear irrelevant for teachers' work. In education in South Australia we have a strong record of teachers' action research, of theorising practice, and of teacher inservice programs built on reflective practices and classroom inquiry. Teachers' and students' workplace investigations are practical means of making connections between theory and practice. The studies in this book are intended as examples of the exploration of theory in practice with a particular interest in language and learning.

The background to preparation for this book is the arrival in South Australia in the past two years of a large number of immigrants, many of whom are refugees from some of the world's most troubled and violent regions. Teachers and school administrators have been challenged by students from violent and discordant backgrounds, some without formal education. Behaviours, cultural knowledge, and literacies, which we take for granted in Australia, become transparent when teaching students for whom the tacit is unfamiliar and the obvious is strange. The circumstances and actions of newly arrived students pose challenges to accepted ways of teaching, to behavioural management, to curriculum designers and to assessment procedures.

In talking with teachers and managers about schooling New-Arrivals I have realised that many colleagues face related challenges teaching disaffected and disturbed mainstream students. The learning experiences of individual students and of groups of students are vastly different. Yet, the difficulties of New-Arrivals and the disaffection of local students both direct attention to the cultural role of schools and the function of formal education in the acculturation of people into valued and privileged ways of going about things in Australian society. A cultural perspective on learning, which explains learning as a social phenomenon, gives insights into schooling success as well as into the sometimes conflict-ridden behaviours of students and into the responses of teachers and schools to such behaviours.

A class of students working with a teacher in a particular subject build or form a community. The concept of a class as a dynamic community provides a coherent framework for probing teaching and conditions for learning. What makes the class a community is the pursuit and development of shared understandings and ways of doing things together. People form communities through interactions in working towards common goals. New students of science, or computing, or English language or electronic engineering work with experienced teachers in apprenticeship roles in order to develop the skills and knowledge which mark out membership of a science community, a community of computer geeks, an English-speaking community, or an engineering community. Through participation in joint activities learners gain insights into and skills in discipline-specific practices. This is the theme of the first essay. It outlines a theoretical framework for investigating pedagogy, curriculum and policy. The framework accounts for learning in general. It is designed to serve as a practical explanation of learning in different contexts.

The following essays provide insights into different aspects of socialisation. A number of ideas link the essays. The first centres on learning to mean. People learn meanings for participation in society through engagement and involvement in community practices. The personal meanings we make of life experiences frame our senses of self or identity (Simon Eddy's essay) and construct our cultural understandings (Fiona Ryan's essay).

A second theme concerns the influence on learners' participation and interest of types of tasks, topics, materials and associated discourses (Mi-ok Lim's essay, Glenda Inverarity's essay, Johanna Motteram's essay). A third theme is the authenticity of activities such as reading (Dongjin Kim's essay) and the use of authentic texts for analysis (Ray Adams' essay).

The essays provide some perspectives on people's meaning-making practices. They are also practical examples of socialisation—in this case into a research community of applied linguists. The essays demonstrate students' apprenticeship into research procedures. The students formulated research questions, collected and analysed data, and documented the experiences in reports. They engaged in social practices using the semiotic resources of researchers to address significant issues and questions. The authenticity of applied research created conditions for students' socialisation into professional practices. For students starting out on research, the essays provide examples of procedures for the study of issues in local contexts. For teachers the essays suggest ways of exploring experiences which are part of their workplace practices.

Overview of contents

Socialisation, social practices and teaching

Peter Mickan

Peter Mickan develops the idea of learning as a social phenomenon. The essay critiques traditional teaching which segregated language from social contexts with subsequent changes in pedagogy which represented attempts to recontextualise language. A social perspective on learning views schooling as the induction of learners into the practices of new communities. Learners develop an expanding potential for living in changing social ecologies using the semiotic or meaning-making resources of the communities. Socialisation is a process of participation in social practices with learners developing understandings and uses of the semiotic resources such as language, tools and behaviours of communities.

Extensive reading *for EFL students in Korea*

Dongjin Kim

Dongjin Kim's paper documents a significant change in teaching English in a private school in Korea—the introduction of *Extensive Reading*. The focus of *communicative language teaching* (CLT) on spoken language sidelined reading in language pedagogy. The studies Kim refers to make a strong case for the value for language learning through extensive reading of books written to entertain or inform. In foreign language contexts, where teachers are not confident in oral communication, Extensive Reading is a practical strategy for learners to develop oracy and literacy proficiency. The paper provides a model for introducing Extensive reading into classes anywhere.

Discourse of the language classroom in Korea

Mi-ok Lim

Mi-ok Lim examines the teaching practices in a secondary school in Korea and compares textbook, teacher-directed discourse with intervention lessons built around *authentic texts* and tasks. Lim provides a valuable introduction to a social view of language and learning. She examines classroom data from the perspective of socialisation. The paper provides a framework for the analysis of socialisation processes in language and in subject-specific classes.

Plumbing the depths of identity transitions in an ESL classroom

Simon Eddy

Simon Eddy addresses a topical issue in the ESL industry—the role of identity in learning. He examines the concept of identity as a tension between 'being' and 'becoming' through the analysis of language use in a secondary school class in Australia. He suggests that the notion of multiple identities blurs identity and that *New-Arrivals* to Australia need to maintain a grounding in their origins for a sense of continuous being. The study provides helpful conceptual frames for consideration of identity of learners from different cultures.

Developing professional phraseology: a corpus linguistics approach

Ray Adams

Ray Adams proposes strategies for the use of concordancing programs in teaching discourses. The paper addresses the significant issue of learners' need to develop discourses specific to technical or specialised social practices. By grouping types of texts specific to a discipline to form a corpus, *concordancing* programs are used to study the structures and patterns of language use. The paper outlines the use of concordancing programs for teaching tertiary students.

Developing local-content material for a New-Arrivals program

Glenda Inverarity

Glenda Inverarity describes steps in the development of a content-based unit of work for ESL students new to Australia. The students attend classes in a centre for teaching adult immigrants. The topic of the unit is related to settlement needs—the Adelaide rental property market. In an action research process the materials are developed, trialled with students and modified after taking account of students' responses to the materials. In the unit students worked with *authentic texts* relevant to their settlement. The paper illustrates cycles of reflective practices applied to materials development.

Aboriginal patients and non-Aboriginal health professionals talk—some issues to consider

Fiona Ryan

Fiona Ryan studied communication between Aboriginal patients from remote communities and non-Aboriginal health professionals. Basing her analysis on previously recorded data, Fiona identified discourse differences between health professionals and patients, differences which stem from different concepts of health and illness. The analysis points to the need for health professionals to learn about their own communication practices and, through action research, to investigate the extent of shared knowledge between Aboriginal patients and practitioners in order to improve communication.

Why won't they talk? An investigation into learner reticence in ESL classrooms

Johanna Motteram

Johanna Motteram considers the topic of *learner reticence* and its causes. The data for the study comes from observation of an intermediate level ESL class, in which the teacher was using a textbook for structuring lessons. Johanna examines the influence on learners' participation of factors such as textbook tasks, topics, oral interaction and learners' comprehension of instructions. The study suggests explanations for *learner reticence* are to be found in the social circumstances of a class community.

A pragmatic approach to editing and publishing at tertiary level

Ioana Petrescu and Judith Timoney

In the final chapter Dr Ioana Petrescu and Judith Timoney describe the context and procedure for editing the contents of this book. They highlight a general theme of the book, which is the value of students' involvement in authentic practices. The students edited the articles for publication, which required adherence to professional standards.

As with postgraduate students of Applied Linguistics, they learnt specialist skills from participation in the social practices of a professional community. Dr Petrescu and Ms Timoney conclude with practical advice for students' academic writing.

Socialisation, social practices and teaching

Peter Mickan

In this chapter I will consider applications of socialisation theory to teaching. Schools are important socialisation settings. Children and students attend schools and universities to learn to participate in the social practices of selected communities. They learn the use of resources such as language, space and material objects for living together and for working with community members. Teaching engages learners in the use of resources for involvement in the practices of communities.

A beginner joining a golf club needs to learn how golfing is done. Golfing is identifiable by a variety of semiotic resources, that is, resources and tools people use to make sense or meanings together in order to play golf. For example, golf clubs and balls are tools, a golf course is the material space, rules of the game are the metaphorical representations of regulated behaviour and playing the game is the physical act of golf. Each of these components combines to create golf as a social semiotic (Halliday 1978), that is, a cultural resource for human beings to do things together on a golf course.

The example of golf illustrates a range of semiotic resources which community members must understand and use to play the game. These resources include:

- the material: understanding the use of club and ball
- the spatial: understanding the layout of the course and movement through the course
- the physical: understanding of body movement for using clubs and balls
- signs of numeracy: recognising the scoring and sequencing of holes
- signs of language: following spoken instructions and explanations of rules, and conversing to maintain relationships and to play together.

All of these are carried out through people's ability to make sense of the system of meanings connected with the game of golf.

Without understanding the system of meanings of golf, or of Australian Rules Football, or of T-Ray biosensing, we can not follow what experienced players or engineers do. When we do not understand cultural meanings we signal that we are outside of the community and we voice our incomprehension: 'I don't know what's going on! This doesn't make sense. I don't understand the rules.' How people understand and use cultural resources determines how they participate in society—in their relationships, work and leisure. One of the main roles of schools is to teach students to capably use a society's cultural resources. For this they need to develop the ability to adopt new practices, to adapt acquired social practices, and to contribute to the creation of practices for sustainable relationships and environments.

Language is a fundamental cultural resource. People's ability to use language lies at the heart of human activity. We conduct many of our practices with language, which maintains and renews cultures and communities. In schools students learn the essential cultural resources of literacies—learning to use the texts and the tools for handling spoken and written language. The use of language by newcomers to Australia is crucial for well being, for contributing to and partaking in society. Language education has a prominent role in preparing Australian and immigrant children and adults for cultural participation.

Language teaching over the last forty years has been characterised by change (Mickan 2004). Forty years of teaching English to immigrants to support their settlement in Australia has contributed to significant changes in curriculum design, teaching activities and assessment. Central to the changes has been the selection of the unit of analysis for curriculum design, for instructional activities and for assessment. Traditional language teaching chose grammatical items and vocabulary as units for instruction. Language acquisition was explained as a process of accumulating linguistic items and a knowledge of how to use those items. Over a number of years students learnt grammatical rules and applied the rules in written exercises as a prelude to communication in the target language. After the Second World War many immigrants to Australia came from *non-English speaking backgrounds*. Adult immigrants did not have years to learn English. They needed language skills in their daily lives.

Immigrants' need to communicate in English on arrival in Australia motivated a search for effective teaching approaches relevant to settlement. The need to communicate launched languages education into a series of transformations, from dealing with language as decontextualised objects to working with language as cultural resource and system for making meanings. Harris (1981) referred to traditional linguistics as the language myth, which decontextualised language and segregated it from context. It was around concepts of communication, cultural contexts and making meanings that language instruction changed.

Situational English was a first step in changes in *English as a Second Language* (ESL) programs designed to meet the immediate communication needs of immigrants. Dialogues were devised to imitate the practical uses of English in specific situations such as banks, post offices and shops. But memorising dialogues proved problematic because of the artificiality of the dialogues and the unpredictability of spoken exchanges, even in set situations such as the post office and bank. Situational dialogues did not prepare learners for variations in language use.

The introduction of functional-notional syllabuses was the next significant change. Based on speech acts such as *to invite, to greet,* or *to refuse,* programs built around functions and notions gave significant insights into actual uses of language, of how we achieve specific purposes with a selection of speech acts. Speech acts, however, are realised through different linguistic choices. A child's refusal to carry out a request may be expressed by physically running away, by saying 'no!', by making other assertions—'I have to do my homework', 'I don't want to'. Matching linguistics selections to social functions was problematic. Besides, just as with situational English, communication continued to be analysed as a linguistic activity.

Communicative Language Teaching (CLT) and more recently task-based teaching added the need to learn meanings as well as forms. Through activities and tasks the approaches generated activities which enlivened students' language use, but it continued to distinguish form from meaning, adding information gap and problem-solving tasks to inventories of grammar exercises and rules, functions and notions, and situations. Recently, genre-based teaching, based on an analysis of language using systemic functional grammar, has been promoted for teaching ESL in Australia. The orientation of a genre-based approach is on the social functions of language and the specific choices made to achieve specific purposes. In contrast with previous approaches teachers and students work with whole texts such as reports, narratives and recounts, which are integrated with contexts of use. However genre-based teaching in practice attends to the language of texts at the expense of the social purposes for which we use language.

Changes in the teaching approaches sketched above represent stages in the recontextualisation of linguistic items, which were originally extracted from social contexts of use for the purposes of analysis and instruction. The approaches added situations, notions and functions, speech acts, activities and tasks in the attempt to authenticate language. But the process of adding elements to authenticate language was flawed. Linguistic analysis continued to be the focus of instruction, with grammar separated from human action, giving rise to a series of basic dichotomies: separation of language from culture, form from function, exercises from use, sentences from texts, language from meanings, the cognitive from the social, and text from context. We do not experience these dichotomies when we speak and read and write. The dichotomies deconstruct our experiences of doing things with language, experiences of using language almost unconsciously as we go about routines and business on a daily basis. In a more substantial way traditional language pedagogies misrepresented the task of teaching by overlooking and neglecting language as a human resource for making meanings.

Language is a natural part of our behaviour because it is one of our means for understanding people, for being understood by others, for representing the world and for getting things done together. This is more than the psycholinguistic analysis of the negotiation of meanings in *second language acquisition* (SLA) studies and in task-based teaching, which identifies negotiation as different linguistic moves such as clarification, repetition and rephrasing. Language is a social semiotic (Halliday 1978), a system of signs which gain significance and meanings in human encounters. Learning a language is learning the meanings of signs and learning to select and use the signs in human endeavours. Each human encounter is an event with possible meanings. The fact that we understand meanings of companions and make sense of their texts and they comprehend our texts is the result of multiple engagements with language in use.

These observations are commonsense, and yet their implications for pedagogy are significant. The social turn in languages education (Block 2003) signals a shift from teaching decontextualised language to teaching language in use. Although language teachers might argue that in traditional pedagogy this was the case, the assumption was that meaning resided in the word rather than in people's construction of the word based on prior experiences of human action. The dismemberment of language and its removal from context in traditional language teaching stripped it of its social meanings and functions. Context is a 'part of discourse not a setting for it.' (Harris 1998, p. 105). The ability to use language grows from taking part in the social encounters of a culture. This is a process of socialisation.

Social practices and socialisation

Socialisation locates learning in people's engagement in social practices (Schieffelin and Ochs 1986). The current interest of SLA researchers in *sociocultural* theory (Kramsch 2002) signals reframing language teaching as socialisation, in which 'contextualization is central to all aspects of signification.' (Harris 1996, p. 145). We develop the meanings of what we say and write through the actions we engage in with other people, be it in physical contacts or in reading a book or looking at an artefact—the cross or a road sign or the guillotine. Cultures comprise different semiotic modes—physical, material, spatial and symbolic—for people's conduct of practices in society. Learning practices is learning to use the semiotic resources of communities.

Signs require people to signify—to make meanings, an active and even confrontational experience. In traditional teaching, language exercises made no sense at all. Sentences were strung together with no coherence. Grammatical transformations of present tense into past tense, or active voice to passive voice made even less sense. Such exercises disregarded the social purposes of using a passive voice to conceal actors, or of the past tense to report an incident in the past, seriously distorting the very nature of language use. In order to do such exercises students did not need to understand the wordings or make selections from the lexicogrammar for the expression of meanings. A social framework places people's meanings at the centre of experience, with language as a vital resource for expressing meanings.

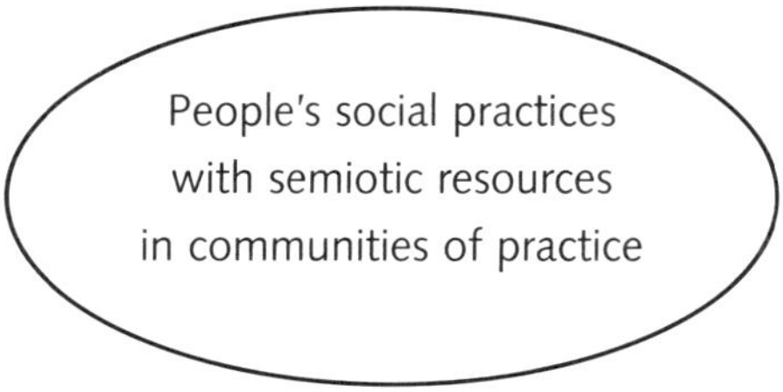

People's social practices
with semiotic resources
in communities of practice

Figure 1. Human action in communities

People's engagement in social practices is situated culturally in place and time. At the moment I am drafting this paper on my computer using technology to express meanings with words and diagrams. The social practice is writing for publication. The semiotic resources I am using include computer with word-processing program as tool, space with visual representation using figures and text on pages, and discourses of applied linguistics. The community setting is lecturer in the University of Adelaide. The language I am using is framed by the particular social practice of an applied linguist writing the introduction to a book for teachers and students. Hence the choice of expressions connected with language education.

Social practices are human acts of people in communities. We observe practices as explicit behaviours and actions and we learn to understand them implicitly in our communication. Social practices as units of analysis for examining human behaviour have specific characteristics:

- Social practices are constituted by people in community. People develop them through and for joint action in relationship with one another. Cultural and historical in origin, they are not separable from human understanding and involvement.
- Social practices are multiple, interrelated, multimodal, and ever changing as they are renewed in human encounters.

- Social practices are situated in time and place as they involve human engagement. As semiotic events, participation in them requires understanding and comprehension of what is going on. People attribute cultural significance to them according to functions in society. Without records of meanings connected with past practices, archaeologists have to speculate about the significance of artefacts, drawings and buildings.
- People's engagement in social practices integrates physical activity, cognitive processing and the material world. Human orientation in social practices is always towards the meanings of experiences and actions, towards making sense of the past, of the present and of the future.

Engagement in social practices with other members of a community nurtures people's understanding of ways of doing and saying.

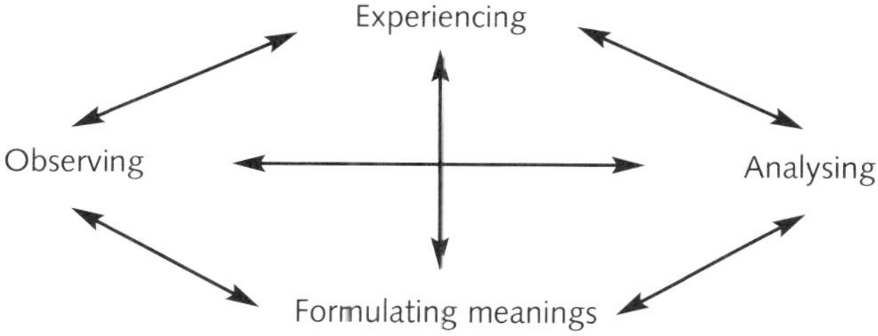

Figure 2. Learning meanings of social practices

Socialisation in a first language envelops children in many, connected practices with primary carers and their communities. The ongoing intricateness of relationships amongst carers and children and practices builds shared ways and meanings for doings things. From repeated encounters with language, children build meanings of the discourses and artefacts surrounding them, exploiting them to expand action into new settings with new discourses. It is the meaning making potential of the language system (Halliday 1985) which makes possible the growth and transfer of language resources into new domains and new communities.

People create communities through their use of tools and discourse conventions, through habitual behaviours and planned activities. Science students learn to use material objects in the physical context of laboratory experiments. They use texts that characterise scientific inquiry: scientific hypotheses; research questions and objectives; diagrams with research instructions and procedures for the conduct of inquiry; keeping records of field or laboratory activities; documentation in laboratory reports and scientific articles (Mickan forthcoming in *Language Awareness*). Students become members of a science community through reading activities.

Prior experiences are the foundation for new, value-laden social practices. The transition from newcomer to experienced community member is a complex series of adjustments and negotiations. This is not simply transmission of skills and know-how by experienced members to less-experienced members. Instruction may lead to conflict as conventions collide with expectations. Transitions involve transformation processes as experienced members adjust to behaviours of new members and negotiate and instruct in response to new members' needs. In this sense a community is permeable and plastic with potential for new meanings and new ways of doing things.

Figure 3. Interplay of social practices across communities

New-Arrivals to communities bring a wealth of experiences and familiarity with many semiotic modes from membership of other communities. Over time they increase their semiotic resources for participation in the practices of new communities. In the process they contribute to shaping communities and society.

Social practice pedagogy

Growing up is learning to take part in ever-widening sets of social practices as we move into new communities through childhood, schooling and adult lives. Education in one sense is the institutional induction into new practices as children enter new social domains. This is apparent in levels of education as children transit from childcare, to junior primary, to primary, to middle and to senior secondary stages of schooling. In each stage children are introduced to new tasks with different resources and practices. Instruction focuses on the development of specialised skills so that by the time students take school leaver courses they are engaging in specialised programs of science, or mathematics or legal studies, or physical education or historical research. In each case the subjects in a curriculum are constituted by the technical acts, tools and discourses which circumscribe people's roles and functions in society.

The social practice framework has general application to education and training across subjects and domains. Social practice pedagogy has six defining characteristics:

- Membership: The goal is membership of communities with shared practices.
- Resources: People function in communities with semiotic resources, including material, spatial, physical and symbolic resources.
- Socialisation: Members learn the meanings and the use of resources of communities from assisted participation in social practices.
- Awareness: Instruction assists new members' engagement in social practices through selected consciousness-raising activities in the use of semiotic resources.
- Design: Curriculum is structured through the identification and analysis of communities' social practices and the semiotic resources for the conduct of those social practices.
- Transformation: Communities change and transform with entry of new members and through adaptations to cultural changes.

Social practices are practical units of analysis for curriculum design, for instruction and for research. They are empirical. From birth we are included in social practices as acts of relationship with carers. We observe, we take part in, we plan, we create and we teach social practices. For instruction, teachers select practices appropriate to the prior experiences of students and build on them. Language teachers choose language-mediated social practices, that is, those that depend on language for realisation. For the enhancement of comprehension, teachers select practices which are multimodal with physical, material, and visual modes underpinning the linguistic. Selection enables teachers to target practices appropriate to different learners. For beginners, teachers choose social practices with multiple semiotic resources—visual, linguistic and sounds—to facilitate comprehension. For experienced learners, choices include complex texts.

A school or university class forms a social group that over time develops characteristics of a community. A defining characteristic of a community is a common interest in working together, with people developing shared understandings and use of semiotic resources for realisation of goals. This is central to a learning theory of socialisation. People develop use of semiotic tools or resources of a community to do things together. The capacity for people to work together is signalled by their ability to use shared resources: knowledge of how things are done, skills for doing things, language for collaboration and for passing on knowledge and expertise in problem solving for maintenance and renewal of communities.

Schools comprise many communities and the placement of children and students in particular lessons and subjects creates environs for socialisation into specialised practices. Apprenticeship in a class or in another workplace involves beginners or those at the periphery moving towards mature or experienced participation in practices. A new class is marked by institutional conventions and the teacher's task is to develop the resourcefulness of individual class members through participation in practices so that together shared goals can be attained. As with apprenticeships in general this is a combined endeavour of students and teacher developing valued ways of doing things, with the teacher modelling and scaffolding the technicalities for working in concert.

Socialisation involves communities and newcomers in processes of adjustment and transformation. Refugees and non-English-speaking immigrants are experience rich, familiar with multiple social practices gained in learning to live in different communities, in some instances learning to survive in hostile and hazardous relationships. Prior experiences of social practices enable newcomers to make transitions for living in Australia, although many practices may be unfamiliar: practical everyday acts to do with accommodation, with banking, with education and with travel. Newcomers may possess strengths of resilience, resistance and independence, characteristics well suited to survival in a competitive society. Personal strengths of self-determination, individual resistance, and expressions of opposition may challenge practices and values in school. But contestation creates opportunities for negotiation and reciprocal transformation, as new and established members adjust practices to work together.

Curriculum design

Curriculum design typically begins with the identification of communities and their cultural purposes. These are described in schools as content subjects. The content of the curriculum is based on the description, selection and analysis of social practices that constitute communities together with the semiotic resources which sustain them. Instruction centres on planned encounters in selected practices, including highlighting typical features of resources essential for participation (Mickan forthcoming in *Language Awareness*). A curriculum designed for immigrants new to Australia is based on an analysis of the social practices essential for citizenship. Initial selection focuses on practices for meeting immediate needs. For language programs the selection includes practices which are language mediated.

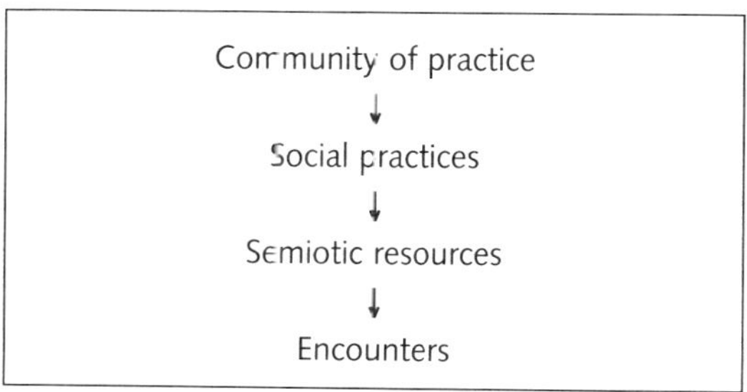

Figure 4. Designing curriculum

Curriculum creates conditions for entry into technical and specialised domains of culture—language teaching, sport, science, filmmaking, and creative writing. The aim is for learners to become skilled in the practices of teachers, of footballers, of scientists and of artists, and skilled in the language of their professional practices. Apprentices learn through encounters with social practices. Apprenticeship is learning to mean with the technical resources of professionals at work in specific domains of society.

A curriculum designed for language development is constructed around the texts of social practices. One of the characteristics of language use in daily life is its patterned nature. We rely on the regularity of language use to select what we say and anticipate what our interlocutors say. We communicate with oral and written texts. Texts enable participation in practices. A shopping list sequenced in the order of items to be purchased at different stalls in the Adelaide Central Market metaphorically represents shopping logistics or plan of purchases. A diary with listed appointments signifies physical meetings, tasks and actions. Our everyday language use is so embedded in practices that it is usually below our level of conscious attention. The interwoven character of social practices, overlapping across communities, complicates the identification of particular or discrete social practices for instruction. Selection of texts for instruction is based on the social purposes of the texts.

The curriculum model prioritises language as focus for participation in practices. Text types are aligned with purposes of practices. The selection procedure integrates human action with the purposes for which we use language.

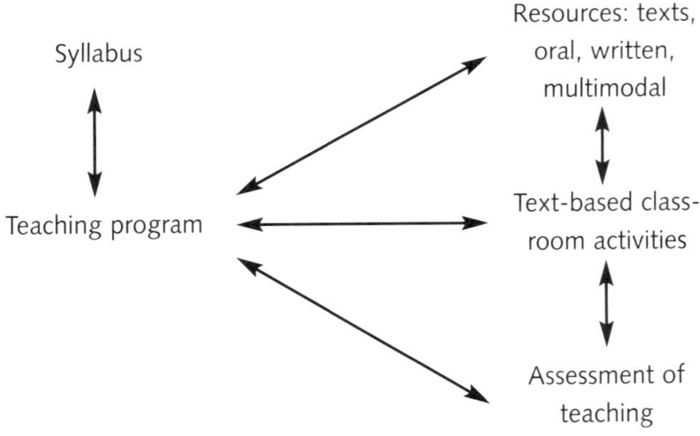

Figure 5. Curriculum components for language-mediated practices

Teaching the language of social practices

For teaching, as for the curriculum, the motivating question is: what practices do children and students need to learn for membership of communities? Socialisation in formal education is heavily dependent on language, with education systems carrying responsibility for the development of literacy skills for cultural participation. Language instruction framed by social practices privileges the development of skills in understanding and communicating with texts. The specific identification of the lexicogrammatical or discourse features that characterise social practices is the focus of attention.

A social practice perspective recognises learners' familiarity with discourse conventions from their primary language experiences and builds upon learners' meaning-making resources from prior experiences. Cultures share social practices, which permit cross-cultural communication. Languages share discourse conventions and language behaviours. The study of narratives across cultures depicts shared generic structure expressed in particular wordings and sequences of occurrence. The procedure for planning instruction is to determine learners' familiarity with discourses.

Characterise target community
Determine learners' prior experiences
Select social practices and semiotic resources
Model encounters with practices
Assist learners' analysis and use of resources
Support learners' independent participation

Figure 6. Planning instruction

At the forefront of language choices are people's practices. Language and practices are mutually constitutive. Language is one of the sign systems for making sense of, and for taking part in, community practices. Text types or genres characterise particular practices. Teachers assist students' in noticing discourses for participation in practices by selecting and highlighting formative features.

Adopting a social practices frame of analysis situates language learning in human activity. Classes form communities characterised by practices and use of semiotic resources. The normal activities of a class offer scope for socialising students in the use of different discourses. Class work is authentic and relevant to the functioning of the community. Lessons are environments for apprenticing learners into specialised discourses (Mickan 2006). Teachers' actions and teaching activities provide texts for learners' observations of human action and resources for action. The patterned, ordered sequencing of teacher instruction, of class behaviours and of lesson content directs learners' awareness to significant conduct and valued meanings. Recordings of lessons and analysis of transcripts provide insights into students' opportunities for learning discourses for participation in practices. Teachers and students' awareness of language choices for specific purposes is raised through analysis of language use.

Directing learners' attention to characteristic features of texts challenges traditional grammar teaching, which taught syntax out of context, divorced from use and focused on rules of usage. Language is a system for expression of meaning potential. Within a socialisation paradigm teaching the language of social practices is carried out through raising awareness of the specific language choices constituting texts. Teachers instruct students in the selection of patterns of language use, for the expression of targeted meanings in the context of practices. Teaching awareness of language use and language choices in texts assists students' use of appropriate discourses for independent, community participation.

Investigating social practices and further reading

This essay has been written to provide an integrated framework for the analysis of learning, for teaching and for research. A research program will investigate applications of concepts to formal and informal learning environments. To study social practices and their semiotic exponents is not easy, given the complexity and interrelatedness of social practices in communities. Socialisation is inherently unstable and unpredictable as well as sustaining and systematic. What is clear is that it is not possible to isolate and identify social practices in the way gene-carrying DNA sequences of the honeybee, the fruitfly and the mosquito have been decoded. Peoples' participation in practices of communities is dynamic as are their understandings and uses of semiotic resources.

The suggestion in this paper is that a focus on social practices as units of analysis provides a practical and integrated way into the study of instruction and learning. The task is to address questions raised by this framework. These questions include minimally the following:

- What is a community of practice? Does a school class constitute a community of practice?
- What social practices comprise and define communities?
- What are the social practices we engage in and what are the language conventions for participation?
- What systematic procedures are there for investigating semiotic resources of practices which are by definition not finite?
- What systems for analysis enable classification of social practices and their semiotic resources, including the text types of practices?
- What is the nature of instruction in different settings where teachers apply social practice pedagogy?
- What insights into learning and research into learning does the framework generate?

Suggested reading

The references listed below are suggestions for further study. I have found the ideas of the authors especially helpful for thinking about learning, for doing research and for teaching linguistics.

Language theory

Halliday, M 1985, *An introduction to functional grammar*, Edward Arnold, London.

Halliday, M 1978, *Language as social semiotic: the social interpretation of language and meaning*, Edward Arnold, London.

Halliday, M & Hasan, R 1985, *Language, context and text: a social-semiotic perspective*, Deakin University Press, Geelong: Victoria.

Harris, R 1981, *The language myth*, Duckworth, London.

Harris, R 1996, *Signs, language and communication: integrational and segregational approaches*, Routledge, London.

Halliday, MAK 1978, *Language as social semiotic*, Edward Arnold, London.

Social semiotics

Hodge, R & Kress, G 1988, *Social semiotics*, Polity Press, Oxford.
Lemke, J 1990, *Talking science: language, learning and values*, Ablex, Norwood, NJ.
Van Leeuwen, T 2005, *Introducing social semiotics*, London, Routledge.

Socialisation and second language acquisition

Block, D 2003, *The social turn in second language acquisition*, Edinburgh University Press, Edinburgh.
Kramsch, C (ed) 2002, *Language acquisition and language socialisation*, Continuum, London.
Schieffelin, B & Ochs, E 1986, 'Language socialization' in *Annual Review of Anthropology* vol.15, pp. 163–191.

Communities of practice

Lave, J & Wenger, E 1991, *Situated learning: legitimate peripheral participation*, Cambridge University Press, Cambridge.
Wenger, E 1998, *Communities of practice: learning, meaning and identity*, Cambridge University Press, Cambridge.

Social paradigms of teaching

Hasan, R & Williams, G (eds) 1996, *Literacy in society*. Longman, London.
Toohey, K. 2000, *Learning English at school: identity, social relations and classroom practice*, Multilingual Matters, Clevedon.
Unsworth, L 2000, *Researching language in schools and communities: functional linguistic perspectives*, Cassell, London.
Wells, G 1999, *Dialogic inquiry: towards a sociocultural practice and theory of education* Cambridge University Press, Cambridge.
Wells, G & Claxton, G 2002, *Learning for life in the 21st century: sociocultural perspectives on the future of education*, Blackwell, Oxford.

References

Block, D 2003, *The social turn in second language acquisition*, Edinburgh University Press Edinburgh.

Halliday, MAK, 1978 *Language as social semiotic: the social interpretation of language and meaning*, Edward Arnold, London.

Halliday, MAK, 1985 *An introduction to functional grammar*, Edward Arnold, London.

Harris, R 1996, *Signs, language and communication: integrational and segregational approaches*, Routledge, London.

Harris, R 1998, *Introduction to integrational linguistics*, Pergamon, Kidlington: Oxford.

Kramsch, C (ed) 2002, *Language acquisition and language socialisation*, Continuum, London.

Mickan, P 2003, 'Beyond grammar: text as unit of analysis' in *Grammar in the Language Classroom: Changing Approaches and Practices*, J. James (ed), pp. 220–227, SEAMEO Regional Language Centre, Singapore.

Mickan, P (in press) 'Doing science and home economics: curriculum socialisation of new arrivals to Australia' in *Language and Education: An International Journal*.

Mickan, P 2006, Socialisation through teacher talk in an Australian bilingual class, *International Journal of Bilingual Education and Bilingualism*, vol. 9, no. 3, pp. 42–358.

Mickan, P 2004, 'Teaching methodologies' in *Teaching English in Australia: theoretical perspectives and practical issues*, ed C Conlon, API Network, Australia Research Institute, Perth, WA, pp. 171–191.

Teramoto, H and Mickan P (forthcoming) 'Writing a critical review: reflections on literacy practice' in *Language Awareness*.

Extensive Reading for EFL students in Korea

Dongjin Kim

Extensive reading for pleasure is used in Korean elementary schools as part of Korean literacy classes. Teachers, parents, the school community and students agree it is important to improve Korean literacy in young learners. However, in an English class in Korea, no one realises or emphasises the importance of extensive reading for pleasure even though many involved in *First Language* (L1) learning focus on the importance of reading.

Huge amounts of money and energy are poured into learning English. A news article reported that Koreans spend about $US4 billion a year learning English through private tuition, reference books and learning English overseas (*Dong-A Daily*, 4 February 2002). Schools fail to encourage students to enjoy learning English and build their language proficiency. Students care so much about the *Test of English for International Communication* (TOEIC) and *Test of English as a Foreign Language* (TOEFL) scores that they study in private institutions to achieve a good result.

TOEIC was originally developed from the *Educational Testing Service* to assess Japanese business people's English proficiencies. Thus, the characteristics of the test are very much business-oriented. Oral language proficiency and writing skills are not assessed in this test and it solely consists of multiple-choice questions.

TOEFL is designed to evaluate candidates' English proficiency for those wanting to study at universities in English-speaking countries. The context of the test is academically-oriented and although essay writing and oral interviews have recently been added to the test, examinees still prefer multiple-choice style testing.

There are various benefits for those who achieve a high TOEIC or TOEFL result. Middle school students with good scores are able to attend better high schools. Recently, students who scored well in English in the University Entrance Exam or who had a higher score in TOEIC or TOEFL were at an advantage when applying to well-known universities. When applying for a job or within employment, TOEIC or TOEFL results can play a crucial role in securing further employment or a promotion. This reveals why young students and middle-aged business people spend most of their time learning English in an uninteresting setting unsuited to their age.

Regardless of the enormous investment in learning English, especially for these two tests, news reports have revealed and highlighted the problem with the *English as a Foreign Language* (EFL) teaching approach in Korea. *Dong-A Daily* reported that Korean applicants were ranked sixteenth out of twenty-three Asian countries on the new style TOEFL, which includes essay writing. Another news article reported that a manufacturing company was delighted to employ a student who had scored 980/990 on TOEIC. When the new employee was sent to the Trading Department, the company was shocked to discover he could not conduct business with their English-speaking trade partners (*Dong-A Daily*, 19 February 2002).

According to Mickan (2004), English continues to be taught through grammar translation and situational English. These two teaching methodologies are also adopted in TOEIC, TOEFL and school tests. The blend of these two phenomena, that is, no awareness of reading for pleasure and test-driven English teaching, causes a lack of interest and poor language proficiency in Korean students studying EFL. Different teaching strategies and methodologies should be taken into consideration and a much more dynamic style of teaching is needed in order to interest EFL learners and improve their language proficiency. *Extensive Reading* is one possible solution for exhausted students learning English in Korea.

Extensive Reading

An extensive reading program was implemented in a private English institute in Ulsan, Korea. This action-research program was designed primarily to get students interested in reading English books. Both at home and school there are no books available for students to read except those used for grammar study. The idea of the program was to implement *Extensive Reading* to try to interest students in reading for pleasure, either in a class setting together or individually.

The project was conducted over ten weeks from July to October

2004. The classroom library was set up and a lesson plan was designed for the program. Initially ten students joined the course but during the program some students left while others joined.

An introduction to Extensive Reading

Extensive Reading involves reading a wide range of details, ideas, or items and also typically involves 'reading massive amounts of very simple material so that the learner can read smoothly, confidently and pleasurably. The focus is on general comprehension, and not directly on language practice' (Waring 2004). In this report, *Extensive Reading* is incorporated as one of the teaching strategies for L1 and *Second Language* (L2) learners.

The benefits of Extensive Reading

Nation (1997) pointed out a number of benefits of an extensive reading program. First, it is important that students read at their own pace and level. They do not have to necessarily commit to a fixed *curriculum*; it can be flexible enough to accommodate students with diverse language proficiencies.

Students experience less pressure when studying English and interacting with others. They choose books of their own interest and decide what to read by sharing their reading experiences with their peers, teachers or family. Teachers or parents can guide students' reading by suggesting proper reading levels for them, by pointing out the various text types a student may be interested in. Another merit of this program is that students can read whenever and wherever they want: the L2 learning process continues outside class.

One problem in teaching English in Korea is that many Korean English teachers lack confidence when conducting lessons in English. It is obviously desirable for teachers to speak fluent English. However, in practice, teachers, regardless of their own language proficiency, tend to use grammar-based teaching methodologies for the reasons outlined earlier and also because it is easier to deliver than *Extensive Reading*. *Extensive Reading* requires a lot of class preparation and resources and generally, Korean teachers teaching subjects other than English do not use a variety of teaching methodologies. Thus, for EFL teachers there is the problem of language proficiency as well as the lack of skill in presenting and organising lessons in an interesting way. The benefits of *Extensive Reading* allow willing teachers with low English proficiency to conduct new class language activities.

Grammar-based teaching methodologies, popular in Korea, concentrate on each word and sentence structure and do not allow for overall meaning in texts. This means students get bored and frustrated easily and have poor English proficiency. Mickan (2003, p. 226) confirms this view saying:

> In a reversal of traditional teaching, which extracted language from context and dealt with meaningless and emaciated linguistic objects, text-based teaching begins with social contexts. Learning is socialisation into the meaning making systems of another language, but based on learners' experiences of making meanings ... Second language learning is learning to mean, using textual resources of the second language for making meanings. The literate activities and discursive practices implicit in working with texts initiate and apprentice learners into the social meanings of the languages they are learning.

Extensive Reading is a good way to incorporate text-based teaching. In other words, by introducing *Extensive Reading* principles we can utilise different types of texts such as multimedia or written text, and text-types such as informational, narrative or procedural text for classroom activities (Butt, Fahey, Feez, Spinks & Yallop 2003; Mickan 2003). This enables learners to understand beyond the word and sentence level of English. By reading different texts they can acquire or learn different characteristics of the language. This learning activity leads learners to language learning through a meaning-making process rather than a grammar-based style. These associated class activities, in conjunction with *Extensive Reading*, improve reading and also enable students to explore different aspects of the language such as speaking, presenting, debating, book reviews and discussions in class.

In large classes, especially within the public school system, *Extensive Reading* and the associated text-based activities allow students to work and read at their own level as well as providing a more stimulating learning environment. This learning process has another benefit —students can continue their reading outside class. To accomplish this, teachers can give homework requiring students to read a certain amount of text, or set a goal for reading within a time period. Students can also prepare presentations for class at home.

Young learners can be encouraged to read using rewards such as a merit system.

It is important to note that little research has been carried out with Korean EFL pupils (Neyman 2002). However, the benefits of *Extensive Reading* as a teaching strategy have been reported in researches with ESL/EFL learners (Asraf and Ahmed 2003; Elley 1996; Hwang 2001; Nation 1997; Krashen 1993; Day & Bamford 2000).

Lesson plan for the Extensive Reading project

Mickan (2004) reviewed eight different teaching methodologies used over forty years in ESL and EFL teaching. *Extensive Reading* was proposed as one of the literacy practices, with *talk around texts* and *shared books and reading aloud* as classroom activities. Mickan's teaching strategies were adopted and rearranged for the *Extensive Reading* project. Using *Extensive Reading* as the main teaching strategy, and mixing other literacy practices as sub-teaching strategies, allowed the use of many other teaching methodologies in the program. As a teaching strategy, *Extensive Reading* can adopt text-based teaching such as content-based teaching and genre teaching (Mickan 2003; Feez 2002).

The lesson was planned to include reading, writing, listening and speaking in various class activities. The four language skills are combined in each activity and the primary focus of the lessons is to reduce stress and make the content interesting and fun (see Figure 1). In lesson plans, students begin with the read-aloud sessions to motivate them to read books and read in their own time. The link between the different activities and skills is illustrated in Figure 1.

Reading and writing

Students listened to the teacher read in class. They borrowed books to read at home or in class on their own during *Sustained Silent Reading* (SSR). Using the English dictionary, students read English explanations to find meanings suitable to the context.

Students wrote book reviews and kept vocabulary books. Generally, because students are used to filling in blank spaces with multiple-choice answers, they are not accustomed to writing freely or expressing their own ideas and opinions. Sample book reports and vocabulary books were provided as a guide.

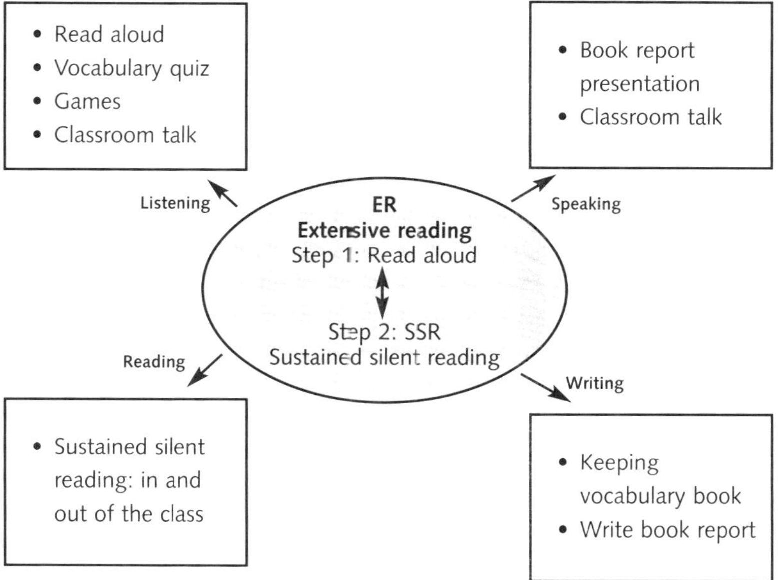

Figure 1. Model of Extensive Reading basic lesson [adapted from Mickan (2001)]

Speaking and listening

When they finished reading a book, the students wrote a review in their book reports and presented it to the class. By doing this, they practised speaking English in front of other people. Vocabulary games, sentence relays and question and answer games in English were included to improve verbal English.

When reading aloud to the class, the teacher asked the students questions about the text, pictures or their own views. This enabled a natural dialogue to develop between the students and teacher. As a result the students lost their self-consciousness and were eager to participate.

Method

There were three main objectives of this study. Firstly, to document the implementation of the *Extensive Reading* Program in Korea. Secondly, to evaluate students' responses to *Extensive Reading* and finally, to discuss the implications of teaching the program in Korean EFL classes.

School

The project took place in an industrial city on the south-eastern coast in Korea. The school is a franchised private English institute with about eighty students in the new and modern inner-city area of Ulsan. The *curriculum* is based on teaching English through reading English books. The problem with the program is that the Korean authors, who write books for students studying English, emphasise grammar teaching through reading. To a certain degree some of the books have interesting stories but the issue is that sentence structure is artificial when compared to *authentic English texts* and books are not used for reading for interest. Instead, they are used as texts for comprehension practice and translation work. What little interest the narrative may hold is quickly dissipated by the onerous and repetitive study and dissection of a text and students become bored after one or two years of study. 'Even if they are avid readers in their first language ... all too often they do not become readers of English' (Day 2000).

Students

For this study, the students who joined the program were aged twelve to fourteen years. The students were at varying levels of proficiency with some highly motivated to learn English while others showed no interest and were forced to study English by their parents. There were ten students in the first four weeks of the class during the summer vacation, four female students and six male students:

Six boys: HK: 12 years, SW: 11 years, KM: 11 years, SY: 12 years, IT: 11 years, JM: 11 years
Four girls: DH: 13 years, HS: 13 years, YE: 13 years, HR: 13 years.

After summer vacation five students left the class because of other school class commitments. Two new students (MW: 12 years and JH: 11 years) joined after the program's fifth week.

Teachers

There were three Korean English teachers working in the school, no native English-speaking teacher, and one Director. None of the staff read English books for pleasure but they did read English reference and textbooks for teaching purposes. The male teacher, SK, who administered the *Extensive Reading* class, had not read any children's books written for native English-speaking readers before. He showed a strong interest in it but at the same time also had concerns about implementing a program to encourage children to read English books, especially those who hardly read Korean books in their free time. He read about twenty percent of the books before the program started. He did not teach the first week of the *Extensive Reading* class but observed the organised classes.

It was decided that simple short stories would be the best option and lengthy discussions determined appropriate books for read-aloud sessions. SK pointed out that easier and shorter books were needed for the students to read for themselves, as longer books would be more difficult for students to read. Before the program started there were more long books than short story books. It was emphasised to the remaining teachers that they should be role models to students and read as many books as possible before or during the *Extensive Reading* program.

The Director was supportive of the *Extensive Reading* program and was willing to buy books for the classroom library and planned to buy ten books every month. In Korean schools, great emphasis is placed on producing copious amounts of worksheets that prove students work hard. Parents like to see lots of paperwork because they believe it validates or proves their child is learning English. The Director was asked not to force the students to read a certain number of books, compel them to finish book reports for every book they read nor add to the vocabulary books. It was crucial to counterbalance the pervading idea by making the *Extensive Reading* program an enjoyable reading environment and experience.

Data collection and analysis

Five different types of data were collected in the study. Table 1 shows data types and research methods of the study. Classroom conversation was audio recorded to examine students' responses in the class activities. In *Teacher's note,* the teacher described lessons and kept records of the students' responses to the lessons bi-weekly for the duration of the project. Book reports and vocabulary books written by students were also checked and students kept book logs about each book they read. In the tenth week of the program, students' feedback was obtained using a questionnaire. All the collected data was examined to see how different teaching methodologies interacted with each other and contributed to the results of the

Extensive Reading *program*

Table 1. Data type and research method (Sit 2003)

Data type	Research method
Classroom conversation	Participant-observation and introspection
Teacher's note	Introspection
Students' work	
– book report	Observation and introspection
– vocabulary book	
Students' book log	Introspection
Students' feed-back; Questionnaire	Introspection

Procedure

Considerable preparation was carried out both in Australia and Korea before the start of the *Extensive Reading* program

Preparation for research in Australia

While preparing for the project in Australia, a local primary school literacy class was observed to obtain ideas and information about setting up a classroom library for the *Extensive Reading* class in Korea. A range of approaches was used to choose books including: observing local children book surfing at the bookshop, talking with others about their book preferences and monitoring read-aloud segments in children's TV shows. Also, other diverse factors were considered for choosing books. A variety of text types was considered, the students' gender, where the books were published and cultural characteristics included in different authors' work. The level of reading difficulty and thickness of books also had to be considered in order to attract young students' interest.

Preparation for research in Korea

While visiting Korea for two months to set up the *Extensive Reading* class, more than a hundred English books were purchased for the classroom library. Half the books were bought in Australia and the other half were bought in Korea, based on the same criteria of book choice.

The selected vocabulary book and the report for the literacy review were found too formal for students to record their reading experiences. With resources from a seminar in Gwangju, Korea in June 2004, as well as Internet searching, the style of the book report was changed to suit young learners (Amer 2003) and vocabulary books were adapted for the class (enchantedlearning 2004).

Extensive Reading program in Ulsan, Korea

The *Extensive Reading* class was conducted both during and after summer vacation. This had little effect on the class and the *Extensive Reading* program.

The Extensive Reading *class during summer vacation*

During the four weeks of summer vacation the class studied for ninety minutes a day, five days a week. I ran the first week of the *Extensive Reading* program and the Korean teacher, SK, took the class for the next three weeks. It was decided SK would conduct the classes as he was quite proficient in speaking English and felt confident about implementing the *Extensive Reading* program. He observed the class for the first week to see how classes were conducted.

The Extensive Reading *class after summer vacation*

After the summer vacation, class time was reduced to fifty minutes a day but students still had classes five times a week. In addition, most students in the *Extensive Reading* program had an extra fifty minutes of classes with the other Korean teachers. These classes were grammar,

Junior TOEIC or lessons with story books provided by the school's franchise (In Korea, most English institutes are part of a number of English teaching franchises that supply their materials including books). These classes were organised by the director of the school and were independent of the *Extensive Reading* program.

Results and discussion

The program greatly benefited the students and produced many pleasing results. Although several improvements could be made to enhance the effectiveness of the program, overall it was deemed a success.

Students' interest in Extensive Reading

Students read more

According to the answers from the questionnaire, five students had read an average of 1.8 books since they started learning English, but after starting the *Extensive Reading* class they read an average of 39.2 books. Figure 3 shows each student's book reading record before they started and after the *Extensive Reading* program. The graph includes the results of five students with ten weeks of *Extensive Reading* classes and two new students with two weeks. The number of books students read increased significantly.

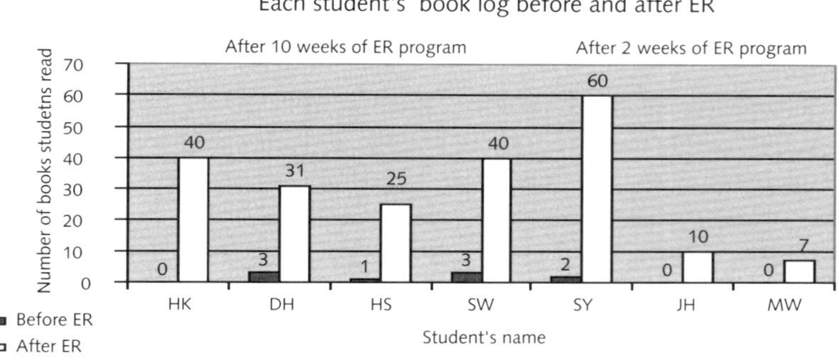

Figure 2. Students' book reading during the Extensive Reading program

Students' attitude to reading changed positively
Before starting the program, none of the seven students were interested in reading English books in their free time. Six students answered that they were not interested because there were no English books around them to read. Interestingly, SY, who read the most books during *Extensive Reading*, answered that he only read English books because his mother forced him. After *Extensive Reading* only one student, HS, showed a negative attitude to reading English books. HS read the fewest books compared to other students, except the two new students. However, in the questionnaire, even HS gave positive feedback saying her writing and speaking improved.

The Extensive Reading *program helped students' English language skills*
Krashen (1993 p. 72) said, 'Writing style comes from reading' and Nation's (1997) comment on the improvement of students' spoken language skills after the 'book flood' are not unexpected considering the literacy activities in classes In the questionnaire, seventy percent of students said they thought *Extensive Reading* helped their writing skills and all students answered that *Extensive Reading* improved their speaking proficiency. The results also represent the students' increased confidence in writing and speaking. This is mainly due to the meaningful input from reading and reasonable practice during literacy activities.

Comparing the 'Top Ten Principles of Extensive Reading'

Day and Bamford (2002)suggested the 'Top Ten Principles for Teaching *Extensive Reading*' for teachers who wanted to examine the use of *Extensive Reading* for their teaching. When implementing *Extensive Reading* in the Korean classroom for young students, these principles were used for the class and to evaluate the results. Table 2 shows the brief evaluation of the ten weeks *Extensive Reading* class in Korea.

Evaluation of principles 1–4
Some of the reading material was too difficult for certain students. Even though there were ranges of text-types in the classroom library, there were more books in the higher level than the lower level of reading difficulty. Some autobiographical and informational texts were

Table 2. Valuation of 'Top Ten Principles for Teaching Extensive Reading'

Top Ten Principles for Teaching Extensive Reading	Valuation
1. The reading material is easy.	✗
2. A variety of reading material on a wide range of topics must be available.	✔
3. Learners choose what they want to read.	✔
4. Learners read as much as possible.	✔
5. The purpose of reading is usually related to pleasure, information and general understanding.	✔
6. Reading is its own reward.	✗
7. Reading speed is usually faster rather than slower.	✔
8. Reading is individual and silent.	✔
9. Teachers orient and guide their students.	✔
10. The teacher is a role model of a reader.	✗

(Successful, ✔: Satisfactory, ✗: Wasn't successful, O)

inappropriate for students with lower reading levels. Learners chose what they wanted to read. Considering HS, DH and HK's reading level and the number of books in the library, these three students read as much as they could but there were not enough books in the library for them to continue.

Evaluation of principles 5–10

Principle 5, where students were told the purpose of reading is often related to pleasure, information and general understanding, worked well. However, Principle 6 was difficult for the unenthusiastic reader. In the early stages of the *Extensive Reading* class, students were rewarded by participating in the reading class, giving their opinion in English, presenting their book report and answering the quiz. But later on the reward system and the reading aloud sessions were discontinued even though they had encouraged the reluctant readers to read (Fox 2001). On the other hand, about the same time the homeroom teacher started to mark students' vocabulary books and book reports, which contradicts Principle 6. This may also have contributed to students' reading record dropping around week five.

During the *Extensive Reading* program students read faster rather than slower to gain a general understanding of the books. Reading occurred privately both at home and in class. Even though the homeroom teacher was the only teacher instructing students in English book reading, it was important and crucial that other teachers working in the institute were also role models for reading (Day & Bamford 2000). In this case many teachers did not read any English books and it was hard for teachers to suggest books to read or talk about books. It was important to encourage students to read and set up a text-rich environment that included the students seeing the teachers read. It is impossible to insist students read when staff are reluctant to do so.

Overview

When we think of an EFL classroom in the school system in Korea, in many cases the classroom is over-crowded with more than thirty to forty students with different language proficiencies. Mostly, students are taught one fixed curriculum to cope with school exams. At the same time the Korean English teachers' language use in the English class is limited in vocabulary and proficiency. There are few native English-speaking teachers to provide a rich verbal language input. The Korean government's plan to have five thousand native English-speaking teachers in public schools by the year 2007 has failed because of the financial expenditure (Joong-Ang Daily, 5 September 2002).

As previously referred to there are many advantages to using an *Extensive Reading* program. Even though all the possible teaching activities associated with *Extensive Reading* were not explored in the relatively short time of ten weeks, the benefits were obvious. However, there were some minor problems. The teacher required training and it became apparent after assessing the data that there were not enough easy-to-read books. As a result some students were unable to continue reading as they had exhausted all the books available to them at their reading level (see Evaluation of principles 1–4). It must be remembered that students had increased the number of *authentic* English books they had read from an average of 1.8 books to an average of 39.2 books in ten weeks.

Fruitful results were drawn from this project. In only ten weeks students started to read English books for pleasure and discovered that reading is not only fun but also supports their language acquisition. It is therefore suggested that further training of teachers is required and an increased variety of books should be available at each reading level. It was also discovered that rewarding students' progress is more encouraging than marking or inspecting their work, a notion not widely encouraged in the Korean teaching system.

This study shows how one of the possible and practical applications of *Extensive Reading* encouraged young students in Korea to enjoy and acquire skills for reading, writing and speaking English. Many meaningful texts helped students to develop English skills in literacy, not with pressure but pleasure.

References

Amer, A 2003, 'Teaching EFL/ESL Literature' in *The Reading Matrix,* vol. 3, no. 2, viewed 8 August 2003, <http://www.readingmatrix.com/articles/amer/article.pdf>

Asraf, RM & Ahmad, IS 2003, 'Promoting English language development and the reading habit among students in rural schools through the Guided *Extensive Reading* program' in *Reading in a Foreign Language,* vol. 15 no. 2, viewed 8 August 2003, <http://nflrc.hawaii.edu/rfl/October2003/mohdasraf/mohdasraf.html>

Butt, D, Fahey, R, Feez, S, Spinks, S & Yallop, C 2003, *Using Functional Grammar: An Explorer's Guide,* National Centre for English Language Teaching and Research, Macquarie University, Sydney.

Day, R and Bamford, J 2000, 'Reaching Reluctant Readers' in *Forum ENGLISH TEACHING,* vol. 38 no. 3, viewed 10 August 2003, <http://exchanges.state.gov/forum/vols/vol38/no3/p12.htm>

Day, R and Bamford, J 2002, 'Top Ten Principles for Teaching Extensive Reading' in *Reading in a Foreign Language,* vol. 14, no. 2, viewed 17 August 2003, <http://nflrc.hawaii.edu/rfl/October2002/day/day.html>

enchantedlearning.com 2004, *Vocabulary Map Graphic Organizers,* viewed 11 June 2004, <http://www.enchantedlearning.com/graphicorganizers/vocab/index.html>

Elley, W 1996, 'Lifting Literacy Levels with Story Books: Evidence from the South Pacific, Singapore, Sri Lanka and South Africa', International Literacy Institute, <http://www.literacyonline.org/products/ili/pdf/ilprocwe.pdf>

Feez, S 2002, *Text-based Syllabus Design,* Macquarie University, Sydney.

Fox, M 2001, *Reading Magic,* Pan Macmillan, Melbourne.

Hwang. SK 2001, 'Reading Skill Development of an ESL Student: A Four-Year Longitudinal Study' in *Korea TESOL Journal*, vol. 4, viewed 8 August 2003, <http://www.kotesol.org/pubs/journal/2001/abs_sang.shtml>

Krashen, S 1993, *The power of reading*, Libraries Unlimited Inc, Englewood Colorado.

Mickan, P 2003, 'Beyond Grammar: Text as Unit of Analysis' in *Grammar in the Language Classroom*, ed EJ Joyce, SEAMEO Regional Language Centre, Singapore, pp. 220–227.

Mickan, P 2004, 'Teaching Methodologies' in *Teaching English Language in Australia: Theoretical Perspectives and Practical Issues*, ed C Conlan, APINetwork, Australia Research Institute, Curtin University of Technology, Perth, pp. 171–191.

Nation, P 1997, *The Language Learning Benefits of Extensive Reading*, <http://www.jalt-publications.org/tlt/files/97/may/benefits.html>

Neyman, PF 2002, 'Helping Children Learn to Think in English Through Reading Storybooks' in *The Internet TESL Journal*, vol. 8 no. 8, viewed 2 October 2003, http://iteslj.org/Articles/Neyman-Storybooks/

Sit, MK 2003, Singlish – threat and threatened, BA Hons thesis, University of Adelaide.

Waring, R 2004 What is extensive reading?, viewed 12 May 2004, <http://wwwl.harenet.ne.jp/~waring/er/er_faq.htm>

Appendix A

Students completed the questionnaire in Week 10.

Questionnaire:

1. How long have you been learning English?
2. Do you like reading Korean books?
3. After *Extensive Reading*, do you like reading English books? Why, why not?
4. How many English books did you read before the *Extensive Reading* class, except textbooks?
5. How many English books, except textbooks, have you read now?
6. Do you enjoy the read aloud sessions?
   If yes, why?
   If no, why not?
7. Did you like to read English books in your free time before you joined the *Extensive Reading* class?
   If yes, why?
   If no, why not?
8. Which English classes do you prefer: *Extensive Reading* classes or normal classes? Why?
9. Before the *Extensive Reading* classes what was your interest level in learning English?
   ☐ Not interested ☐ Interested ☐ Very interested
10. Now after the ER classes what is your interest level in learning English?
    ☐ Not interested ☐ Interested ☐ Very interested
11. Do you think reading a lot of English books through *Extensive Reading*, helped your writing?
12. Do you think reading a lot of English books through *Extensive Reading*, helped your speaking?
13. Do you want to continue the *Extensive Reading* classes?
14. Do you have anything else you want to say about *Extensive Reading* classes?

Discourse of the language classroom in Korea

Mi-ok Lim

This study discusses an investigation of current English teaching practices at a secondary school in Korea. It includes a critique of Korea's public English *curriculum* for Year 8 classes, and explores how the *curriculum* is realised in textbooks and classroom discourse and practices. In the study, text-based teaching is applied in addition to traditional English teaching practices, as a suggested alternative method of teaching.

The study attempts to answer the following: What is the nature of the classroom discourse of the traditional secondary English class in Korea?; How is it different from that in the intervention lessons when the text-based teaching method is applied?; What theories inform the current secondary English *curriculum*, textbook and teaching practices?

Learning English in Korea

Korean parents are highly enthusiastic when it comes to their children learning English. This is partly due to the fact that the English component in the *College Scholastic Ability Test* (CSAT) is worth as much as one quarter of the total score, and also there are a large number of companies recruiting more employees who can speak and write English fluently.

The CSAT was first administered in 1993 as a replacement to the National College Entrance Exam. In the CSAT, English reading and listening comprehension questions were introduced, while grammar and vocabulary questions—which had been tested in the previous national exam—were excluded. The 2004 CSAT English test included seventeen listening comprehension questions as compared to eight in 1993 and thirty-two reading comprehension questions. The number of listening comprehension questions has increased significantly since 1993. This increase reflects the nation's growing interest in English communicative proficiency, also stated in the Seventh National Curriculum which took effect in February 2000.

In 1997, Korea's Ministry of Education issued a public notice on the Foreign Language Education Curriculum. The *curriculum* places emphasis on the development of communicative proficiency in English teaching, and the reform resulted in changes to English teaching methods and textbooks.

English teachers

The low success in English learning at public schools in Korea is partly due to the low level of English proficiency and teaching skills of the teachers. Only a small percentage of English teachers in Korea are found to be competent to communicate in English (Arirang 2001). Therefore, English teachers are currently under pressure because of increasing societal and governmental demands for better English and teaching skills.

The English Curriculum

The English Curriculum, which is part of the Foreign Language Education Curriculum, is divided into courses: *English, English I, English II, English Reading, English Conversation*, and *English Writing*. The *English* course is compulsory for primary (Years 3–6) and junior-secondary (Years 7–10) education, while the other courses are optional at senior-secondary level. The sections of the *curriculum* include: Nature, Objectives, Teaching Contents, Teaching and Learning Methods, Evaluation Methods, and the Appendix. In the Appendix are lists of recommended subjects, communicative functions, vocabulary, and example sentences sorted by grammatical categories.

Secondary school English education aims to enhance students' comprehension and ability to produce everyday English, and help students establish sound views and values through understanding the values and culture of the countries where English is spoken. The teaching methods at secondary school are required to maintain students' interest in English, further develop basic skills for communicating in English, provide activities to improve both fluency and accuracy, and maximise learning experiences. According to the *curriculum* statement, the teaching methods must relate to the language learning process (Ministry of Education 1997, pp. 26–27). Details of teaching methods are specified in the Teaching and Learning Methods section of the English Curriculum.

In contrast to traditional, teacher-directed lessons, the Seventh Curriculum requires learner-centred instruction based on tasks. Reviewing the content of the previous lesson is considered necessary for the internalisation of content, which will result in producing natural expression. The *curriculum* requires teachers to focus on the four language skills: listening, speaking, reading, and writing. Specifically teachers should actively:

- use audiovisual materials to teach listening comprehension and natural language
- provide meaningful and communication-based speaking practice to improve both fluency and accuracy and to develop students' creative use of language
- teach fast-reading comprehension
- replace sentence-by-sentence translation with writing a short text around students' own ideas.

English is the recommended language of instruction. The Teaching Contents section specifies that communicative activities should be organised around the functions and notions listed in the Appendix (Ministry of Education 1997, pp. 27–28).

The English textbook for Year 8

In the classroom observed, the teacher's main teaching resource was the textbook chosen by the school's organising committee. This was the main resource because teachers are too busy with additional administrative work to design their own teaching materials. Secondly, the English teacher observed takes just one of the eight Year 8 classes, and another teacher has the other seven. The other English teacher decided to give written tests for all Year 8 classes, so for fair assessment, the two teachers agreed to base the test mainly on the textbook contents. This practice is common in schools when there is more than one subject teacher sharing the same year-level classes. Finally, students have paid for the textbook so the teacher needs to make the best use of it.

The textbook is composed of twelve chapters, and each chapter includes practice of listening, talking, reading and writing skills. A chapter starts with a cover and title, a picture, a guessing section, learning objectives, and a list of communicative functions and example sentences. Learning objectives and functions are written in Korean while the rest is in English.

Transcripts of audio dialogues for listening practice are attached at the back of the textbook. The dialogues were created around the five communicative functions allocated to the chapter. The transcripts can be easily recognised as artificial creations because they contain no repetition, false starts, or hesitations that normally appear in daily conversations. In talking activities, students are mostly engaged in conversations and role-plays using sentence examples.

The reading section is composed of warm-up questions in Korean, a written text with new word pronunciations and their meanings—also written in Korean—and comprehension questions at the end of the text. Writing activities include practising the passive voice and some expressions, and writing a news report following a given example. The chapter finishes with questions about two written texts containing passive voice, a game designed to practise *-ing* and *-ed* forms, and two more activities for learning the passive voice.

On the basis of this chapter, the textbook was designed around communicative functions and points of grammar. Even though each chapter has sections for practising four linguistic skills, they are all geared towards repeating and internalising structure and grammar.

Existing language classroom research

Language classroom research began in the late 1960s, when researchers found the results of comparative research into teaching methods inconclusive (Allwright & Bailey 1991). Allwright and Bailey (1991, p. 18) argue that language learning 'happens, when it happens, as a result of the reactions among the elements that go into the crucible [classroom]—the teachers and the learners.' Classroom discourse is therefore considered as the central means through which learning takes place, because it constrains or empowers students' participation and thinking (Hicks 1996; Johnson 1995).

Cho (1998 p. 74) argues that the limited success of Korea's educational reform is partly due to the lack of understanding of the 'venue for education', the classroom. In Korea, classroom research has been limited and mostly experimental in nature, and there is hardly any research by Korean teachers (Cho 1998). It seems that teachers in Korea are uncomfortable with having observers in their classrooms, even it provides a great opportunity to reflect on their own and others' teaching practices. Lim (2003) argues that often there is a mismatch between Korean teachers' perceptions of their classrooms, and the findings from classroom transcription data analysis. Finally, previous research has only dealt with turn-taking patterns, and generally has not considered subject content.

Social view of language and learning

This study is largely informed by the theory of language as a meaning-making resource, the sociocultural perspective of language, the social practice view of language, and the socio-cognitive theory of learning (Halliday 1978; Lemke 1993; Heath 1983; Ochs 1988; Ochs & Schieffelin 1984; Rogoff 1990 Wertsch 1991; Mickan 2004; Vygotsky 1987). According to Halliday (1978, p. 2), 'A social reality (or a "culture") is itself an edifice of meanings—a semiotic construct', and language is one of the most distinctive *semiotics* because 'it also serves as an encoding system for many (though not all) of the others.'

Researchers from a *social semiotics* perspective are interested in how community life is constructed with signs (Lemke 1993). In *social semiotics*, meaning is viewed as an active process generated through social interaction, and therefore as a social relation (Walkerdine 1982). This perspective contrasts with that of *formal semiotics*, which only looks at the systematic features of language in making sense of meaning.

Communication requires participants' ceaseless work to interpret the text at a particular moment, in light of the context, because 'there is no absolute meaning of a text' (Firth & Wagner 1997; Olson 1991, p. 19). The meaning, as Rommetveit (1983, p. 18) argues, is decided on 'what at the moment of utterance is taken for granted by both conversation partners.' In Volosinov's (1973, p. 102) terms:

> Meaning does not reside in the word or in the soul of the speaker or in the soul of the listener. Meaning is the effect of interaction between speaker and listener … It is like an electric spark that occurs only when two different terminals are hooked together.

We make sense of a text not only on the basis of the *lexical* items and the grammatical structure, but also through the *contextualisation cues* (Gumperz 1982). These include 'pitch, stress, intonation, pause, juncture, proxemics (distance between speakers, spatial organization [*sic*] of speakers), eye gaze, and kinesics (gesture, body movement, and physical activity)' (Gee & Green 1998, p. 122).

However, it is the *lexical* items and grammatical structure that have been the main concern of psycholinguistics and formal *semiotics*, without recognising the significance of the paralinguistic features of communication. Therefore, in the traditional lessons influenced by psycholinguistics, word meanings and language use have been considered as 'the constructed system of elements removed from their practices and community of users' (Hall 1995, p. 209). A word or a phrase is considered as having one absolute meaning that cannot be changed or modified. Lesson activities in the traditional lesson are dominated by grammar explanation, and memorising the spellings and meanings of L2 words and phrases in the students' L1. The texts are designed for achieving lesson goals, mostly at the elementary level.

Apart from the immediate paralinguistic *contextualisation cues*, interaction is mediated by the socio-historical elements of the participants such as 'gender, social class, race, religion, and geographical region, … and other social and professional groups' to which people belong (Hall 1995, p. 215). This is because people's linguistic and paralinguistic choices differ according to social backgrounds. When children learn a language they are ' "socialised" [*sic*] into the value systems and behaviour patterns of the culture through the use of language at the same time as he [*sic*] is learning it' (Halliday 1978, p. 23).

Recent research influenced by Vygotsky's sociocultural theory, has started to emphasise the social nature of learning, including L1 and L2 learning, and the social relations and roles among the participants in interactions leading to learning. Johnson (1995, p. 133) considers the learning process as 'enculturation ... into particular ways of making sense and perceiving their experiences ... [and] acquiring new cultural frames of reference'. Lave and Wenger (1991), drawing on the social view of learning, claim that learning takes place when the learners move from 'legitimate peripheral participation' to full participation in the class community. Therefore, 'participation is both the goal as well as the means of learning' (Kong & Pearson 2003, p. 88).

To view learning this way is not to isolate the learning process from the social context, but regard it as 'relations among people in activity in, with, and arising from the socially and culturally structured world' (Lave & Wenger 1991, p. 51). Schieffelin and Ochs (1986, pp. 167– 168) argue that becoming a full participant in a community entails knowing the community's language 'by acquiring knowledge of its functions, social distribution, and interpretations in and across socially defined situations.' L2 learners viewed from this perspective are seen as 'new comer[s] beginning to participate in the practices of a particular community' (Toohey 1996, p. 553). New community participants would learn the language through socialisation, or participation in the community's joint language-mediated events and activities. Just as language is social in nature so is learning.

The classroom as a community

A classroom is a community in which learners and the teacher, as members, act upon a shared and unique semiotic system. In language lessons, participants are engaged in ordinary classroom communicative practices as well as interactions around the intended *curriculum*. According to Hall (1993, p. 149) these practices are considered

> powerful forces of group socialisation and learning', because 'they have within them the fundamental temporal, spatial, and social units that underlie the social system of a group, and are the point at which the social and the individual come together and mutually shape each other.

Students should be socialised into their school community by the second year of middle school (equivalent to Year 8). From seven years of schooling, students would have good knowledge of the nature of school life, their roles as students, behaviour rules, and the oral and written communicative practices they are required to demonstrate. In the course of enculturation into the L2 classroom, students are also socialised into the culture of the target language (Johnson 1995).

Learning in the language classroom

There are many students and teachers who strongly believe that language cannot be learned in classrooms. However, if children can learn at least one language in such a small community as the family, then why not in the classroom? The language classroom provides opportunities to practise language according to different social roles. To learn how a socially more powerful person speaks to a less powerful person—and vice versa—students can observe how the teacher speaks and how students respond. Interaction between people of the same social power can be learned through peer interaction.

Just as community actions occur and recur following certain rules and conventions, so do sentences (Lemke 1993). 'A great deal of discourse is more or less routinized [*sic*] ... ' (Halliday 1978, p. 4). Therefore the explicit teaching of conventionalised resources in a group would facilitate new members' socialisation (Hall 1993; Vygotsky 1978; Wertsch 1991).

In the language classroom, particularly for beginners, the community operates primarily around the semiotic system of learners' L1, with minimal use of the target language. Therefore, the *pedagogic* goal of the language classroom is to lead learners to formulate a shared semiotic system of the new language with the teacher, and later in communities where the language is used in social practices. Since language has a social function, learners should be given opportunities to use the target language for social purposes, for the development of their socialisation and language use (Painter 1989).

Research shows that in classrooms where English is the L1, L2, or a foreign language, communication is dominated by the *Initiation, Response, Follow-up* (IRF) structure (Nystrand 1997; Lin 1999a, 1999b; Console 2000; Duff 2000; Hall 1997). Students' participation in and learning from classroom events largely depends on classroom communication patterns, which are heavily determined by the nature of the teacher's Initiation and Follow-up moves (Johnson 1995). Anton (1999) for example, demonstrated how the teacher could create a classroom of learning by inviting the class to solve a problem posed by one student, instead of just giving the answer. Nystrand (1997, p. 3) claims that teachers maintain control of lessons through repetition or recitation, and the students engaged in these patterns, often lose enthusiasm for learning and 'their work is often superficial, mindless, and quickly forgotten.' Students learn better through voicing their own understandings, thereby elaborating their interpretive framework (Nystrand 1997).

Research method for the language classroom study

The data for this research was collected in a Year 8 classroom of a public junior-secondary school in Dae-jon, Korea, from the middle of

April to the middle of May 2004. The school had eight classes for each year level, with girls and boys separated into different classes. I observed, recorded, and transcribed a total of twelve lessons. I intervened during the course of the lessons when the circumstances allowed. There was no need for official approval to get access to the English classes.

The teacher was female and had two years teaching experience. She studied secondary English teaching at a national university and passed the highly competitive National Teachers Recruiting Exam. The exam included an interview in English worth thirty percent. The teacher claimed that she usually instructed the class in Korean; however, while I was there for data collection, she chose to speak English all the time with some Korean translation. The teacher frequently utilised the English textbook chosen by the school.

The students had three English classes a week. They appeared to have a good vocabulary. Students frequently took vocabulary quizzes, where they gave L1 meanings to L2 words or vice versa. Their scores were counted in their final assessment, which contributes to students' high school entrance. The English assessment also includes results from listening and writing tests, and attitude scores. The listening test is broadcast on national radio, and administered simultaneously across the nation to Year 8 students twice a year. The written test examines students' vocabulary, grammar and reading comprehension, and is based mostly on the textbook contents.

The method for the research is *qualitative*, in that the data includes audio/video recordings and transcripts, teacher and student work sheets, field notes, and interviews with the research participants.

Analysis of language classroom observations

The teacher started each lesson with formal greetings and small talk about the previous weekend or lunch. During class, students, for the most part, sat up quietly in their seats facing the teacher, particularly during whole class interactions led by the teacher. There were some occasions where students laid their upper bodies on their desks; if this happened, the students were asked to sit up straight. Students were not allowed to get up from their seats unless they needed materials from their cabinet.

Most of the texts used in the traditional lessons were from the textbook and the accompanying CD, but sometimes the teacher used popular songs and lyrics. Classroom tasks were usually those prescribed in the textbook with the teacher sometimes adding games. The textbook did not contain *authentic* texts, so for the intervention lessons *authentic* texts were written to fit in with the relevant textbook chapter, the school and social contexts.

Analysis of the discourse in an intervention lesson and a traditional lesson focused on the ideational, interpersonal and textual meanings. The ideational meaning was explored by looking at the process words used by the teacher. One significant difference between the two lessons lies in the number of process words the participants used: 33 different process words were used in the traditional lesson and 61 in the intervention. Most of the processes in the former lesson related to general classroom administration, as in 'write down', 'look at this', and 'listen to the CD'; whereas the latter lesson included processes specific to science, as in 'germinate', 'measure', and 'plant'. This is because in the intervention lesson the texts were relevant to science discourse.

Interpersonal meaning was analysed through the mood types in the classroom talk. Due to the task-oriented nature of the traditional lesson, the teacher frequently used imperatives to give task directions, whereas in the intervention lesson imperatives were built into the task content of a procedural text. Students used the imperative mood to greet the teacher through the student captain in both lessons, to make requests for the teacher to repeat a sentence or a question in the traditional lesson, and for information or help during the intervention lesson.

The teacher used the interrogative mood to carry lessons forward and to check students' comprehension, as in 'Understand?' 'Ok?' and 'Got it?' 'What is …?' questions were used to find out students' knowledge of new words. Students asked many questions about task instructions, exams and quizzes, but just three about the subject content of the traditional lesson.

The teacher's talk did not include many modal verbs for metaphorical meaning, making meanings rather congruent. This is opposed to the metaphorical use of modal verbs or interrogative mood for classroom management, which is a common practice in teaching students up to Year 8 (Christie 2002). In terms of tense, there was no use of the present perfect. This could be because the tense had not been introduced to the students yet, or because the teacher did not have this linguistic skill in command. Also, the teacher's L1, Korean, does not have the present perfect tense.

In both lessons 'we' was used to create the sense of working together. Textual themes such as 'now', 'ok', and 'all right', were used to draw students' attention and to carry the lessons forward. English words or phrases were treated as having absolute meaning, without taking into consideration their context.

Classroom participation

As Cazden (1988 p. 29) claims, the classroom discourse was consistent with the *Initiation, Response, Evaluation* (IRE) pattern: teacher initiation, student response, and teacher evaluation. The classroom conversation, therefore, is dominantly monologic, even though it appears to be dialogic sometimes because students make utterances during class (Nystrand 1997). Students' participation in the classroom talk was mostly in response to the teacher's questions. Questions were often addressed to the entire class and students were expected to answer as a group. The questions usually required only a 'yes' or 'no' answer. Students sometimes appeared to reply 'yes' or 'yeah' to the teacher's question of 'Do you understand?' just for the teacher to move on with the lesson, even when they did not understand. In addition to responding to the teacher's questions, students also participated by repeating after the teacher or the audio dialogues.

Most of the teacher's responses to students were to evaluate their answers, therefore the teacher treated the students as rememberers and learning as remembering (Nystrand 1997). The teacher gave strong recognition to the students' confident, collective answers to questions of word meaning. The class, which actively and collectively responded to the teacher, was generally considered a good class.

In both the traditional and intervention lessons, students' questions were not always answered. Students asked few questions because they feared being judged by the teacher in front of their peers. They would ask questions across the class to the teacher when the noise level was high, if they were confident enough and not fearful of a possible negative response.

The teacher asked many display questions in both lessons to check students' comprehension and control (Heap 1985). The teacher's role, it appeared, was to transmit knowledge embedded in the textbook; the students' role was to listen to and comprehend the teacher, which meant students could not question the information (Wells & Chang-Wells 1992).

There was more dialogue and student participation when the discussion related to task procedure, or exams and quizzes. Students sometimes initiated conversation by making comments about the task instructions, or asking about the time allocated for a performance test, which is usually a word test.

The teacher used *authentic* questions when she asked 'How are you today?' 'Did you have a good lunch?' 'Do you have any special plans to do?'(Nystrand & Gamoran 1997). The teacher also asked genuine classroom administration questions, for example: 'Are you finished?' and 'Who's got them all right?'(Christie 2002). These questions are *authentic* and genuine because there were no predetermined answers. Unfortunately, the questions did not involve complex ideas or concepts.

In the intervention lesson more diverse and longer answers were observed. This occurred when the teacher asked students what experiments they had done in the science class and what the results were. Students expressed their feelings toward the lesson contents, which was rare in the traditional lessons. In this lesson, there was also an unusually long exchange between the teacher and the students, most of which was initiated by students. The topic of the conversation was the teacher's baby.

Meaning-making

When making the seed germinators, students asked questions about the meanings of words and instructions, and sometimes made comments about the task. Lesson objectives were not to learn and memorise new words and their meanings in Korean, so there was less word repetition and discussion in the L1.

In the traditional lessons, word and sentence repetition and grammar explanation constituted most of the discussion. Language beyond the sentence level was not dealt with. The teacher and students were engaged in meaning-making only in regards to task directions or comprehension checks. The texts were artificially written and stripped of context.

In the intervention lessons, students were engaged in natural interactions working around texts. Mickan (2004, p. 194) argues that 'from interactions with others' spoken and written utterances, learners borrow and take over the discourse resources for taking part in material and mental actions themselves.' There were occasions where students started to borrow discourse resources from what they had heard the teacher say. Students tried to make sense of words and phrases by asking the teacher questions in the intervention lessons, whereas meanings of words and phrases were merely provided by the teacher in the traditional lessons.

Overview

Korean students have been socialised to think that learning English involves memorising Korean meanings of English words and phrases, and reciting English grammar in Korean.

Students can competently explain linguistic structure, and give equivalent meanings in Korean to English words, sentences, or texts. However, they are not trained to use the language for communicative purposes.

The nature of the classroom discourse changed according to the nature of the text, the tasks used, and the teacher's questions. Students were more actively involved with the *authentic* texts, tasks and questions.

References

Allwright, D & Bailey, KM 1991, *Focus on the language classroom: an introduction to classroom research for language teachers,* Cambridge University Press, New York.

Anton, M 1999, 'The discourse of a learner-centered classroom: Sociocultural perspectives on teacher-learner interaction in the second-language classroom' in *The Modern Language Journal,* vol. 83, no. 3, pp. 303–318.

Arirang 2001, *News broadcast at 6:00 o'clock,* Arirang TV, Seoul.

Cazden, CB 1988, *Classroom discourse: the Language of Teaching and Learning,* Heinemann, Portsmouth.

Cho, Y 1998, 'A Review on the Recent Trends of Classroom Instruction Research in Korea' in *Education Anthropology Research,* vol. 1, no. 1, pp. 73–111.

Christie, F 2002, *Classroom Discourse Analysis*, Continuum, New York.

Console, D 2000, 'Teachers' action and student oral participation in classroom interaction' in *Second and foreign language learning through classroom interaction,* ed JKHLS Verplaetse, Lawrence Erlbaum, Mahwah, NJ, pp. 91–108.

Duff, PA 2000, 'Repetition in foreign language classroom interaction' in *Second and foreign language learning through classroom interaction,* eds. JK Hall & LS Verplaetse, Lawrence Erlbaum, Mahwah, NJ, pp. 109–138.

Firth, A & Wagner, J 1997, 'On discourse, communication, and (some) fundamental concepts in SLA research' in *The Modern Language Journal,* vol. 81, no. 3, pp. 285–300.

Gee, JP & Green, J 1998, 'Discourse analysis, learning, and social practice: A methodological study' in *Review of Research in Education,* vol. 23, pp. 119–169.

Gumperz, JJ 1982, *Discourse strategies,* Cambridge University Press, Cambridge.

Hall, JK 1993, 'The role of oral practices in the accomplishment of our everyday lives: The sociocultural dimension of interaction with implications for the learning of another language' in *Applied Linguistics,* vol. 14, no. 2, pp. 145–166.

Hall, JK 1995, '(Re)creating our worlds with words: A sociohistorical perspective of face-to-face interaction' in *Applied Linguistics,* vol. 16, no. 2, pp. 206–232.

Hall, JK 1997, 'Differential teacher attention to student utterances: The construction of different opportunities for learning in the IRF' in *Linguistics and Education,* vol. 9, no. 3, pp. 287–311.

Halliday, MAK 1978, *Language as Social Semiotic,* Edward Arnold, London.

Heap, J 1985, 'Discourse in the production of classroom knowledge' in *Curriculum Inquiry,* vol. 15, no. 3, pp. 245–279.

Heath, SB 1983, *Ways with words: Language, Life and work in communities and classrooms,* Cambridge University Press, Cambridge.

Hicks, D 1996, 'Contextual inquiries: a discourse-oriented study of classroom learning' in *Discourse, learning, and schooling,* ed D Hicks, Cambridge University Press, Cambridge, pp. 104–141.

Johnson, KE 1995, *Understanding communication in second language classroom,* Cambridge University Press, New York.

Kong, A & Pearson, PD 2003, 'The road to participation: The construction of a literacy practice in a learning community of linguistically diverse learners' in *Research in the Teaching of English,* vol. 38, no. 1, pp. 85–124.

Lave, J & Wenger, E 1991, *Situated learning: Legitimate peripheral participation,* Cambridge University Press, New York.

Lemke, JL 1993, *Talking science: Language, learning and values*, Ablex Publishing Corporation, Norwood, N.J.

Lim, I-J 2003, 'Classroom Observation of a Korean EFL Teacher's Strategies in a Public Elementary School Context: A Case Study' in *Ohak Yonku/ Language Research*, vol. 39, no. 3, pp. 663–693.

Lin, A 1999a, 'Doing-English-lessons in the reproduction or transformation of social worlds?' in *TESOL Quarterly*, vol. 33, no. 3, pp. 393–412.

Lin, A 1999b, 'Resistance and creativity in English reading lessons in Hong Kong' in *Language, Culture and Curriculum*, vol. 12, no. 3, pp. 285–296.

Mehan, H 1979, *Learning lessons: Social organization in the classroom*, Harvard University Press, Cambridge, MA.

Mickan, P 2004, 'Teaching methodologies' in *Teaching English in Australia: theoretical perspectives and practical issues*, ed C Conlon, API Network, Australia Research Institute, Perth: WA, pp. 171–214.

Ministry of Education 1997, *Foreign Language Education Curriculum*, Ministry of Education, Seoul.

Nystrand, M 1997a, 'Dialogic instruction: When recitation becomes conversation' in *Opening dialogue: Understanding the dynamics of language learning and teaching in the English classroom*, Teachers College Press, New York.

Ochs, E 1988, *Culture and language development: language acquisition and language socialisation in a Samoan village*, Cambridge University Press, Cambridge.

Ochs, E, & Schieffelin, BB 1984, 'Language acquisition and socialization: Three developmental stories and their implications' in *Culture Theory: Essays on Mind, Self and Emotion*, eds. RA Shweder & RA LeVine, Cambridge University Press, New York.

Olson, DR 1991, 'Children's understanding of interpretation and the autonomy of written texts' in *Text*, vol. 11, no. 1, pp. 3–23.

Painter, C 1989, 'Learning language: a functional view of language development' in *Language development: Learning language, learning culture*, eds. R Hasan & JR Martin, Ablex Publishing Corporation, Norwood, NJ, vol. 27, pp. 18–65.

Rogoff, B 1990, *Apprenticeship in thinking: Cognitive development in social context*, Oxford University Press, New York.

Rommetveit, R 1983, 'In search of a truly interdisciplinary semantics. A sermon on hopes of salvation from hereditary sins' in *Journal of Semantics*, vol. 2, pp. 1–28.

Schieffelin, BB & Ochs, E 1986, 'Language socialization' in *Annual Review of Anthropology*, vol. 15, pp. 163–191.

Toohey, K 1996, 'Learning English as a second language in kindergarten: A community of practice perspective' in *Canadian Modern Language Review*, vol. 52, no. 4, pp. 553.

Volosinov, VN 1973, *Marxism and the philosophy of language*, Translated by Ladislav Matejka and I. R. Titunik, Seminar Press, New York.

Vygotsky, LS 1978, *Mind in society*, Harvard University Press, Cambridge MA.

Vygotsky, LS 1987, *Thinking and speech*, Plenum, New York.

Walkerdine, V 1982, 'From context to text: a psychosemiotic approach to abstract thought' in *Children thinking through language*, ed M Beveridge, Edward Arnold, London.

Wells, G & Chang-Wells, GL 1992, *Constructing knowledge together: Classrooms as centers of inquiry and literacy*, Heinemann, Portsmouth.

Wertsch, J 1991, *Voices of the mind: A sociocultural approach to mediated action*, Cambridge University Press, Cambridge.

Plumbing the depths of identity transitions in an ESL classroom

Simon Eddy

The current fashion and appeal to the explanatory power of 'identity' (Lemke 2003) may be accounted for by a simple reference to history. That is, for interminable periods of human existence, rates of cultural change were negligible. Now, we are living in times of cultural change the rates of which mirror our exponential rates of population growth.

Novel situations often challenge our capacities to deal with new people, places and activities; even our capacities to survive. Under these circumstances, many of us question ourselves and our abilities, wondering, perhaps, who we are or what we should be doing. This sort of inquiry is taken to be a concern with *identity*.

Much cultural shift in recent times has occurred through the process of unprecedented numbers of people relocating themselves or otherwise being forcibly dispossessed of their homelands through conflict. They must learn a new language, among many other adjustments, in a new country and culture. Additionally, many of these people must spend years in one or more refugee camps or other provisional situations before making their way to places like Australia.

Many students at the Secondary School of English (where the present study has been centred) have experienced the aforementioned circumstances. This school takes a mixture of refugee, immigrant and international students who are aged in their teens. The class in question consists of boys and girls from Sudan, Ethiopia and Afghanistan.

A detailed account of the extent and implications of students' biographical experiences is beyond the scope of this study. Furthermore, no attempt was made in the research to consider or ask from the students whether they actually thought about 'who they are', supposing the question was relevant to their ages or cultures. Considering, however, the *synchronicity* of change with questions of *identity* (at least as linguists may see them) and that learning a new language in itself may be a significant alteration to habitual patterns of thought the question arises whether it is possible to use concepts of *identity* as a suitable analytical model to coherently describe what took place in their classroom. In particular, are identities negotiated both at the social level with others and internally on the psychological level, with oneself? These questions assume that there are various levels of *identity*. Can our model of enquiry see evidence for this?

Concepts of identity as a theoretical tool

The idea of *identity* embraces social categories such as ethnicity, class, sexuality, culture, race and gender, as well as earlier concepts such as selfhood, personality, soul, psyche and persona (Lemke 2003). There is a historical shift in thinking represented here, from the earlier more unitary (and perhaps more rigid) essentialist[1] perspective, to one where the individual is comprised of *multiple identities* (Miller 1999). Hall (1996, cited in Miller 1999, p. 150) suggests that 'becoming' is more important than 'being'. This 'becoming' unfolds through a continual discursive social engagement. Indeed, Hall goes as far as saying that *identity* is never unified[2] and is increasingly *fragmentary* in a globally connected, yet locally more disjointed, world. This view would fit with the *synchronicity* of change and questions of *identity*.

The aforementioned view does, however, seem to neglect most people's sense that there is continuity to their lives. There is a 'material continuity of bodies and other socially meaningful material constructions across time' (Lemke 2003, p. 2). These bodies carry our biological traits, characteristics and emotional tendencies, which we would generally consider to be a part of an individual sense of *identity* and which may span entire an lifetime. Others suppose that we also 'advertise' (Lippi-Green 1997, cited in Miller 1999, p. 149) or 'express' (Blackledge & Pavlenko 2001, p. 249) our given identities. We have something to 'bring along' to a situation (Koole 2003, p. 7).

Perhaps there is a need in us to feel both a sense of being as well as exercise our abilities to become. It is better to understand 'being' and 'becoming' as two poles on the same field, between which there is an interactive and enlivening tension. *Identity*, rather, is a mediating term between *phenomenological* experience (of biological/cognitive being) and social positioning, based on social conditions (access to resources, opportunities and our powers of negotiation) which are the contingencies of 'becoming' (Lemke 2003).

Positioning, in this context, is understood by Davies and Harre (1990, cited in Blackledge & Pavlenko 2001, p. 249) to be a dialectical process in which participants (who are all observably and subjectively coherent identities), interactively create a shared context or 'story' in which to locate themselves. The way we may try to position ourselves is often contested by others. We must then in some way negotiate our position, or *identity*, in a given context.

Blackledge and Pavlenko (2001, p. 249) define negotiation of identities as 'the interplay between reflective positioning, that is, self-representation, and interactive positioning, whereby others attempt to reposition particular individuals or groups.' Two examples in which negotiation of identities is supposed *not* to hold are worth mentioning here. Firstly, the concept of *identity*, based as it is on an 'individualistic view of the self' (p. 249), may not be meaningful to people in some societies. Yet, if *identity* is construed as concerning the relationship between an individual and their society, individualism is then just a configuration of that relationship, which differs only in degree, where an individual's relationships (*identity*) are influenced by their particular circumstances. Secondly, in some places and times, there may simply be no scope for negotiation: for instance, if we have been imprisoned or dispossessed. Still, under these sort of pressures, we are likely to turn the negotiations and repositioning inwards, a process which to some extent, we are possibly doing daily anyway, as we feel our fears and desires moving us this way and that (Lemke 2003).

Finally, at this point, identities and language are reciprocally constructed (Blackledge & Pavlenko 2001). Positioning and negotiation mostly takes place within the terrain of language, which gives us the means to structure—and study—these pursuits. Our language, in return, is shaped by our human need to *coalesce* our experiences, both internally and externally, into coherent continuities (identities).

Two studies in counterpoint

Koole (2003, pp. 5-8), in a study of multi-ethnic students aged between 12 and 13 in a class in Holland, analyses his data as constituting 'evidence of the reciprocal and interactional character of identity construction'. This is a similar perspective to the 'negotiation of identities' but appears more neutral and less intentional. Koole also uses the term 'footing' which appears to be synonymous with 'positioning'. Thirdly, Koole writes that, 'the roles of the "brought along" and the "brought about" [which are deemed here to be akin to the terms "being" and "becoming"] in the construction of identities remain little investigated. (p. 7). Here is another point of confluence, as may hopefully be seen. The study offered here takes hold of the interactional tension between 'being' and 'becoming' in its analysis of classroom observations. There is an instructive divergence, however, between Koole's study and the present one.

Koole uses Zimmerman's theoretical proposal (1998, cited by Koole 2003, pp. 5-6) that suggests there are *transportable identities*, which are stable states across time and place. These would perhaps relate to a sense of continuous being, or *situated identities*, which entail the shared situation(s) or relevant context(s) that the participants may be interacting within. A further concept is *discourse identity*, whereby *identity* is seen to be constructed by the discourse or activities that participants are engaged in. However, Koole (p. 7) says in his analysis of a portion of classroom activity, that 'Benno assumes the *discourse identity* of "problem presenter", and is ascribed [by the teacher] the identity of "answerer", while the teacher assumes the identities of "questioner" and "explainer"'.

It is the contention here, in response, that what Koole refers to as categories of *identity* are better seen as categories of role[3]. Playing a role in a given situation may be a sincere and genuine interaction. All the same, it does not necessarily imply the levels of emotional investment that interactively negotiating one's sense of self (*identity*) would. A participant is more likely to be emotionally attached to or concerned with the outcome of an interaction if it entails a repositioning that includes or excludes them. As a further example, the participant may also be concerned with interactions which recognise (or notably do *not* recognise) their personal standing. These are matters of *identity*. In the present study, then, such terms or labels as 'problem presenter' or 'explainer' would not be taken as sufficiently (emotionally) charged to be categories of *identity*, although they may be categories of positioning and role.

For Miller (1999), inclusion and exclusion are the main concerns in looking at *identity*. Her study looks at three students over a significant period of time (between two and four years), who start their English language learning under very similar circumstances and at a very similar school to the one here in Adelaide. Miller, on the other hand, was interested in her subjects' transition into mainstream high school. This was a transition for immigrants which spanned the automatic inclusion into the *New-Arrival*, non-English-speaking environment of the ESL school, into an environment where they must mix with native English speakers in their own countries. Those born or already socialised into English speaking countries had more time for status-seeking and the politics of exclusion or inclusion, in the high school. The common ground of the first school helped to build a new *identity* but powerlessness and vulnerability were the results of a lack of proficiency in spoken English.

The aforementioned provides us with a significant point to consider. Certain intensities[4] of *identity* provide the individual with the necessary boundaries with which to exclude others, as a protective barrier against disadvantageous repositioning. Thus, Miller (1999, p. 161) says that for immigrants, building a resilient and acknowledged *identity* is a confluence of 'speaking English, belonging, competing and feeling confident'. An acknowledged *identity* has its respected boundaries and attributes. Likewise, issues of social inclusion and exclusion are a concern for the class under the present study.

Method of data collection

This study was undertaken using participation and observation. This method follows recent trends that have favoured personal and subjective (though verifiable) accounts of researcher participation (Paterson, Bottorff & Hewatt 2003) rather than entirely objective methods. There are advantages to this approach. Firstly, it provides an understanding that does not solely rely on canvassing subjects for explanations. This avoids interviewees giving what they think the interviewer might want or what they think is more socially acceptable. Secondly, subjects may be more likely to trust a researcher who is open to participation. It was considered this would facilitate an insider's view because subjects are likely to feel more willing to reveal processes under investigation (Paterson, Bottorff & Hewatt 2003).

It was made clear to the students that I was available to answer questions, and participants read aloud to me in five or six instances. In response to reading difficulties, I modelled conventional pronunciations or clarified meanings. Helpers, such as bilingual aides and others, appeared to be an ordinary and *intermittent* feature of classroom activity, so there seemed to be no particular attention paid towards the presence of a researcher. Researcher participation therefore was accepted as quite genuine and was not overly influential or disruptive.

An audio recording of events was made on three occasions. This was done in order to collect accurate records of interactions. It was felt that a small visually unobtrusive audio recorder would interfere less with ordinary classroom life and allow the research to proceed without the concern of where to focus a camera. There is perhaps a danger for the camera to intrude between the researcher and the class (Paterson, Bottorff & Hewatt 2003).

Another feature of my research was that it adhered to a form of *abductive reasoning*. This means that it was initiated with as much of an open mind as possible. The questions were to come out of the field of investigation itself. 'Abduction is the process of drawing conclusions that includes preferring one hypothesis over others which can explain the facts …' (Pierce 1955, cited by Levin-Rozalis 2004, p. 9). The present research diverges from this grounding in that; ' … there is no basis in previous knowledge that could justify that preference [for one hypothesis over another]…' (p. 9). In other words, when there are no *a priori* theories to drive a particular line of enquiry. This study does not quite make that claim. Instead, the proposal here is that it was from the interrelationships involved (especially the teacher-student-researcher interactions[5]), that this study emerged. The descriptive models employed were nevertheless latent (*a priori*) within the researcher, most probably in the teacher and, possibly within the students, though not necessarily using the same descriptive form. It is suggested, on this point, that there is a universal human capacity for theories of mind (Mithen 1996). We all have to make assessments about others, involving such questions as who they are, where they are from and what they can do. We all discursively interact on the basis of our apprehensions of others (irrespective of language) and these questions are reflected inwardly towards ourselves. The methodology here pre-supposed that.

This emergent, relational process may be considered semiotic. As a *semiotic, qualitative* enquiry, this study has noticed 'signs rather than facts' (Shank 1995, p. 7), and it is about the relationships of those signs to each other. Education, in Shank's words, is as basic 'as eating and sleeping', The same also applies to the teacher-student relationship, and perhaps even to the teacher-student-researcher relationship.

The process of abduction uncovered what emerged from these temporary, though living (meaningful) interrelationships. Also, the data from this study has been organised according to an *a priori* interpretative system. However, it was unknown beforehand which aspects of that system were going to be utilised. The claim here is that an attempt has been made to build as coherent a description of the verifiable events as possible. The validity of that description is now open to discussion.

The study

The classroom itself was fairly small. There was room enough for twelve small desks and a large teacher's desk arranged in a square, with everyone facing in, toward the middle. A large whiteboard was on the wall behind the teacher. Students' first names were stuck to the front of their desks, along with their country of origin. Five girls and three boys were from Sudan, three girls from Ethiopia, and one girl came from Afghanistan. All were in their middle to late teens. They had been in the class for six months and most were now at an intermediate level of proficiency.

There were quite large and prominent poster-sized student profiles, decorated, with a photo and some written background on each. These were on the back wall. The desk names and posters showed that each student was valued and that there was a concern for some of the fundamental features of their individual identities. A large geographical map of Australia was displayed like a large stamp on the 'envelope' of the front wall. The white board was ready to write 'addresses' on or to display the content of 'letters'. The map, then, quite strongly symbolised the journey (of *identity*) that each student must make. Additionally, on the top edge of the blackboard was a row of Aboriginal batik reproductions[6].

Letter to the 'homeland'

On the second visit, a letter actually emerged. On this occasion, there was a relief teacher and the class was in the library. Students were supposed to be completing some small writing assignment on computers, though most seemed to be perusing their favourite singers' websites. One student, who had been in a refugee camp before coming to Australia, was working on a letter to a friend in Kenya.

> Dear My Best Friend Sarah,
> I hope that you all well with your parents, and I am also okay with my parents, I think that you had been started your school in last January in this year, and I also studies in … School of English, my school teachers are very honest, I need you to join us in this school of ours, because the teaching is going well us we needed, I really miss you as you know, you are my best girl friend, I love you as I love myself, but now I want to work hard at school, and I want you to enjoy your school as I enjoy my school, make sure that you will complete your studies as I will do so here in my future, to complete your studies is the only one in my thinking, when we both complete our university, we will marriage our self, and there will be no worries in our future life, and I hope both of us will be working together, I wish you to be a nurse, and I will be a Government which is the great man of Country as you know, I will be the top of Country, and you will be the nurse, there will be know better than that beautiful of ours.
>
> **BY YOUTH**
> **BOY FRIEND**
> **ENCYCLOPIADIAN**

Here is a document that demonstrates just the sort of journey that the map of Australia symbolised; a considerable journey around the world, a life changing series of events, a negotiation of *identity*. There are a number of levels in this letter on which this negotiation may be seen to be taking place. Perhaps the most central one is towards the student himself. There is recognition of the hard work and change ahead, but there are also signs of the student seeking some sort of grounding or anchorage from which to do it.

The first line reads: 'I hope that you all well with your parents, and I am also okay with my parents'. The relationship with his parents is established immediately and this is the grounding which, through them, he reaffirms. The acknowledgment of his girlfriend's parents, suggests, maybe, that this is a customary position to take in his homeland or if not necessarily, at least it enhances the writer's intentions of linking with ancestry. The line, 'I love you as I love myself,' of course affirms an important and grounding relationship with his girlfriend but also strongly affirms the love of his own *identity*, which at this stage would still seem to be largely untransformed by the perspectives of the English language. It is the suggestion here that the love of self referred to by the writer is at a level considerably deeper than the changes in occupation that he realises he will have to make in order to reposition himself into a new society.

'We will marriage ourself'. This was obviously meant to say; 'you and I will get married'. Correct use of English inevitably tends to emphasise a more segmented view of relationships. One may get the feeling from this letter that the writer remains in a world view where inter-personal boundaries are slightly differently configured.

Upon the grounding of his *being*, or known *identity*, and its continuity from his ancestors to his possible descendants, the writer shows his optimistic energy for negotiating the changes ahead. This letter to his girlfriend, on a broader level, is also about the negotiations to be had with a new society. ' … and I will be a Government which is the great man of Country as you know, I will be the top of Country.' Semiotically speaking, there is a powerful poetry to these words. There is identification on a grand scale here. Native English speakers perhaps forget the potency of the word 'a', because without it, 'Country' becomes identified in a different way—more like the way that Australian Aboriginal people have been trying to show non-Aboriginal Australians; that is, that Country has a spirit or life of its own, indeed, its own *identity*. The young man from Sudan is also adding in his letter that he sees Government as *the* operational aspect of the spirit of Country. Government is what assembles and maintains a national *identity*.

Audio transcript

On the third visit, the class was engaged in a Society and Environment lesson, watching a film made in Australia and set in the 1920s. A tribal man was accused of murder and a small team of police went out to find him, using an Aboriginal tracker. The story, as it happened, was a powerful *allegory* on the negotiation of *identity*. The tracker, firmly grounded in his sense of being, continually refused to bend to the repositioning that the police were relentlessly subjecting him to (e.g. that he was 'just a worthless black slave'). In the end the tracker decisively outwitted the brutal police leader. We read at this point the explanation that the teacher was giving about some of the action. The film was still running, though there was time enough for the teacher's commentary at the same time. The teacher's commentary is as follows:

> See, what he's doing is slowly gaining those white men's respect. That's two people that have said sorry to him already – the old bloke when he had to put the chain around his neck, and he's just apologised because he said, *'nah, he's not tracking, he doesn't know what he's talking about.'* … 'n showed him the subtleties of tracking and gained a new respect for him. And he's just said sorry, too.

Perhaps the teacher is being too assertive in giving her interpretation of events ('See …') and perhaps this would leave little room for students to form views of their own. Yet, given that the class appeared familiar with the discussion of issues (a discussion was proposed at the beginning of the class, though there proved to be too little time), the preferred view here is that the teacher's words demonstrate to the students the type of analysis that may be used to explore human interaction. Given the time constraints, there are a number of possible reasons for the teacher to delve into this analysis.

As she had pointed out, in reference to the video, 'this is a story of racism at its absolute worst.' The students were considered able to identify with the presented racial issues as they were all non-European. They are also still in a vulnerable position, not only internally from trauma or great uncertainty, but also externally. Australian people have generally become more accepting of difference, though, as a nation, may be seen to be ambivalent about it. There are remaining pockets of resistance to *New-Arrivals* (this may even be an understatement considering the political issue of asylum seekers and their prolonged detention). As *New-Arrivals* or refugees themselves, the students in this study may be subject to prejudice/racism. Perhaps the best defence they can be offered against such prejudice is to be shown examples, on the personal level, of people like the Aboriginal tracker. His example is that of someone who has quietly (yet with great intelligence and persistence) resisted the pressures—or attempts at repositioning—of racism.

Additionally, that defence would also benefit from an understanding of the Australian *identity* itself—its nature, its constituent characteristics, and its history. As the 'letter to the homeland' showed, people tend to identify themselves on a number of levels. One of these levels is on the grand scale, beyond the local, to the national. While many native Australians would downplay this aspect, this level is perhaps more important for *New-Arrivals* from other lands. Hence, along with teaching students English, teaching them to identify the Australian character realistically is to give them greater means to negotiate the boundaries of inclusion and exclusion within Australian society.

Here is an example from the beginning of the same class, before they resumed watching the film:

1. **Teacher** They had the Aboriginal man with them because Aboriginal people were known for their tracking to be able to find somebody much more easily than white people. How do you think they did that?
2. **Student** They know with the foot.
3. **Teacher** With the, the footprints.
4. **Student** Yeah.

There was really only the slightest of pauses by the teacher before she guessed what was being referred to by 'foot', and there was only the merest tone of correction about the word 'prints'. Semiotically viewed, here was an obviously engaging story (the film) and the important thing was to allow the flow of understanding to continue unfolding without the interference of acts of exclusion, which may sometimes arise from the position of 'I speak proper English' and 'you can't speak proper English', 'I am correcting you.' The teacher's intent was to be inclusive and to recognise and value the student's transitionary *identity*. It is also a form of negotiation to be welcoming and accept someone's abilities and meaning as they stand at the time.

This final excerpt is taken from the same discussion, just a few minutes after the dialogue about 'the foot'. We can only deal with it incompletely at this point. It represents quite a complex play of both intra-personal *identity* and inter-personal *identity*. The teacher displays some animated curiosity towards some information that two of the students have about the actor who played the tracker in the film.

1. **S1**	I saw this man
2. **T**	The Aboriginal guy?
3. **S1**	Yes
4. **T**	Where did you see him? David Gulpilil
5. **S1&2**	[...]
6. **S1**	Adelaide. Womadelaide.
7. **T**	Ah. Was he at Womadelaide?
8. **S1**	Yes.
9. **T**	You reckon you saw him?
10. **S1**	Yes.
11. **T**	I reckon he might have been there actually. Yeah ... Yeah ... I reckon you're right. Did you talk with him?
12. **S1**	Nah.
13. **S2**	Just saw.
14. **S1**	Singing and ...
15. **T**	He was. You're right. And was he good?
16. **S1**	Yeah, very good.
17. **T**	Ok.

In a way, the teacher becomes one step removed from her role as teacher because of her emotional interest (which she makes clear by the tone of her voice which was still at 'teacher's' volume) in an issue related to her personally (in the boys' information). Her approach to the boys is layered, too. There *is* some level of display (giving a sign) involved. She wants to make it clear that she is sidelining her role as teacher for the moment and that they are to talk out of the bounds of their usual positioning. There is the adult-teenager differential as well but in her efforts to be inclusive this is played out non-*hierarchically*.

The students experienced an emotional progression, from slight uncertainty to (for one of them in particular) quite a full feeling of recognition. Expressed in the tone of voice, he sounded quite confident. Additionally, this exchange gave the class the opportunity to see the deeper *identity* of the teacher. Such moments are a reminder that the teacher is not just a teacher. Teaching is a role that exists in a wider community of organisation. Undertaking that role is a well-recognised way of being included in that community. Playing the role of teacher can be a more flexible approach. It in no way implies insincerity, but allows a grounding or anchorage to the resources of a deeper sense of self, of continuity and *identity*, from which multiple roles may be played. As the exchange achieves its culmination, 'ok', we hear another layer again. Not so much the teacher but the person returning to her role. Reciprocally, the students are signalled that it is time to return to their role.

Overview

This study has looked at the concept of *identity* in just some of its complexities. A central issue has been the tension between 'being' and 'becoming' which we explored through the examination of language used in both written and spoken form. One way of seeing this tension is to say that it is between what we 'bring along' and what we 'bring about'. To further clarify, it can be explained as a *disparity* between who we are (or who we think we are) and what we do.

It is the finding of this study that the notion of *multiple identities* may tend to blur our boundaries too much. That is, *conflate* who we are with what we do. In which case perhaps we do become fragmented and less integrated, considering current rates of cultural change. Looking into the language use of *New-Arrivals* to Australia, however, shows us the likely need that they have for maintaining a grounding in their origins and loving relationships, in other words, in their sense of continuous being—their deepest layer of *identity*. That many negotiations of social positioning, social *identity* and self conception lie ahead for them is undeniable. We may facilitate these transitions by valuing who they are (their deepest *identity*) as much as valuing what they may come to do or say Unless the idea of *multiple identities* can account for the *phenomenological* experience of continuity, then the preference here is for *layers of identity* which can both account for continuity and our experience of personal depth. It can conceptually avoid, furthermore, the fragmentations of *multiple identities*.

Additionally, it is the suggestion here that we need a word that describes the operational relationship between who we are and what we do, in order to keep the polarity between the two clear. That word is 'role'. It has been the stance of this study to consider categories of role to be less emotionally charged than categories of identity. While roles, to varying degrees, are enmeshed within community organisation and practice, they are also positions which are more frequently adopted, transformed, or discarded along with the planned or unexpected discontinuities of those communities within today's world.

A role is a position to take up or assume in which we may fully and sincerely immerse ourselves. Yet it also implies the presence of deeper layers of identity from which we operate upon the roles we enact. The language of *New-Arrivals* shows us that people instinctively plumb the greater depths of their identity, their being, searching for the inner resources to meet circumstances of significant change. From this grounding they may maintain a kind of 'participant-observer' perspective from which they may enhance their learning and resilience in the face of novelty and the need for the adoption of new roles in new lands.

Furthermore, roles are also something that we may *play*. In terms of teaching, playing supposes a greater flexibility of function (what we do) which enables the teacher to tailor their positioning with an ESL student to be more inclusive. To engender a feeling of value and inclusion may very likely enhance learning and negotiations with difficult transitions.

From here, it may be instructive to look more closely at the sort of transitionary language of *New-Arrivals* such as that in the letter that this study examined. Negotiation of *identity* is important for the individuals involved. Could we as an English speaking culture allow ourselves to renegotiate our own cultural *identity* and use of language in response to the *New-Arrival* culture?

Notes

1. *Essentialist*: Containing clearly identifiable properties or characteristics which, to varying degrees, match up to some ideal of the species, type, or (for the purposes of this study) individual.
2. *Identity is never unified*: Interpretations on this point may vary. It is not said that Hall is actually denying the existence of being. It is supposed here, however, that 'being' does imply some degree of unification or integration. Hence, denying unification of *identity* or of *multiple identities*, is denying being, or the sense of it.

3. *Categories of role:* Koole's perspective seems in keeping with the notion of *multiple identities* which, as has been mentioned, conceptually tends to enhance the view that society and its members are becoming more fragmented.
4. *Intensities:* This relates to the emotional strength and habits of thought and behaviour by which an *identity* is maintained.
5. *Teacher-student-researcher interactions:* There are others, such as those including the rest of the school, the wider community and the world, for instance.
6. *Batik:* An art form using wax and dyes on cloth.

References

Blackledge, A & Pavlenko A 2001, 'Negotiation of Identities in Multilingual Contexts' in *The International Journal of Bilingualism*, vol. 5, no. 3, pp. 243–257.

Koole, T 2003, 'The Interactive Construction of Heterogeneity in the Classroom' in *Linguistics and Education*, vol. 14, no. 1, pp. 3–26.

Lemke, JL 2003, *Identity Development and Desire: Critical Questions*, viewed 8 June 2005, <http://wwwpersonal.umich.edu/~jaylemke/papers/Identity/identity-aera-2003htm>

Levin-Rozalis, M 2004, 'Searching for the Unknowable: A Process of Detection—Abductive Research Generated by Projective Techniques' in *International Journal of Qualitative Methods*, vol. 3, no. 2, viewed 10 June 2005, <http://www.ualberta.ca/~iiqm/backissues/3_2/pdf/rozalis.pdf>

Miller, J 1999, 'Becoming Audible: Social Identity and Second Language Use' in *Journal of Intercultural Studies*, vol. 20, no. 2, pp. 149–165.

Mithen, S 1996, *The Prehistory of the Mind: A Search for the Origin of Art, Religion and Science*, Phoenix Paperbacks, Orion Books Ltd, London

Paterson, B, Bottorff, J, & Hewatt, R 2003, 'Blending Observational Methods: Possibilities, Strategies, and Challenges' in *International Journal of Qualitative Methods*, vol. 2, no. 1, viewed 11 June 2005, <http://www.ualberta.ca/~iiqm/backissues/2_1/ html/patersonetal.html>

Shank, G 1995, 'Semiotics and Qualitative Research In Education: The Third Crossroad' in *The Qualitative Report*, vol. 2, no. 3, viewed 8 June 2005, <http://www.nova.edu/ssss/QR/QR2-3/shank.html>

Developing professional phraseology: a corpus linguistics approach

Ray Adams

This chapter discusses a corpus linguistics approach to the development of high-level English writing skills among migrants and international students from backgrounds of other native languages. It is aimed at teachers and future teachers of English language learners (ELLs), especially those learners who may have gained some proficiency in general English, but who require insights into higher level, specialised language used in professional or academic life.

A university student may be required to write essays or a thesis, or publish works in English language refereed journals, and will often face challenges with both general and academic English. The terminologies and structures within the specialised discourses of their disciplines of study, however, present further challenges. These same challenges arise for the migrant professional attempting to engage in the specialised discourses of a chosen vocation, perhaps also needing to write for publication, or for business or technical communication.

Language courses cover many of the everyday genres of English, but they rarely cover the highly specific forms of English that professionals, students and academics need to work, write, study and publish successfully (Swales & Feak 2000). Students often complain that they do not feel confident with their use of English and identify it as one of their primary difficulties in the overseas study experience (Sawir 2005; Swales & Feak 2000; Craswell 1992). It has also been acknowledged that the language used in teaching materials is often contrived for the purpose and not the *real* or authentic language used in the particular fields of study that students embark on (Nelson 2003; Lewis 1994; Tribble 1989). Some courses offer insights into *business English* but this is a broad approach and does not necessarily include the English of the various avenues of business possible in modern society. Business can involve a diverse range of discourses: real estate, mechanical engineering, confectionery manufacture, or any one of a vast number of completely different avenues of business that will each present their own challenges to the *New-Arrival*.

Attempts to cover such a broad array of possible language areas could prove costly and even impossible unless learners can take some responsibility for their own learning. Corpus linguistics approaches offer ways for students to examine authentic texts as used in specialised discourses, but these approaches do not, as yet, seem to have become part of mainstream classroom language teaching. Language teaching organisations and teachers may have a role in providing guidance in the use of *concordancing* and providing access to ready-made corpora for a range of professions and academic disciplines in a self-help model.

Studies using corpus linguistics have shown that certain types of texts, when grouped together in a corpus, can reveal the patterns and structures inherent in that text type (Johns 1994; Stevens 1995; Gledhill 2000). Gledhill (1999b) applies the term *phraseology* to this characteristic of texts and the term *rhetoric* to the regular phraseologies associated with specific subject matter. Other studies have demonstrated similar phenomena when using corpora comprised of discipline-specific texts (Johns 1994; Koyama, Nakano & Matsuura 2003) and have pointed to the value of a corpus linguistics approach in the development and refinement of high-level writing skills in a tertiary study context (Lee & Swales 2006; Thurstun & Candlin 1998).

Research at two universities in South Australia has investigated ways of refining the use of a *concordancing* program as a tool for student use. The studies involved developing discipline-specific corpora and allowing students to conduct text searches on the basis of their individual language learning needs, and use a web-based concordancer for searches of more general language features. The trial groups generally recognised the capacity of *concordancing* as a self-help tool in improving their own academic writing skills, and some participants showed interest in developing their own corpora (Cargill & Adams 2005; Adams 2006).

Concordancing is a tool that has been used for many years to research the structures and patterns of language in use, and more recently to develop teaching materials which can help learners to study and learn about those structures and patterns. The emergence of *concordancing* software for use on personal computers has meant that the tool is now readily available and extremely fast: a teacher or student can search for keywords and find concordances for them as quickly as one might find word definitions in an online dictionary or a dictionary installed on a computer. Johns (1994), Stevens (1995) and others have focused the use of this software on the teaching of structures and patterns within academic genres for ELL students, but the software has so far remained in the control of language researchers and teachers as a means of developing teaching materials or of demonstrating to their students the ways in which language is used.

In terms of the phases and models of *Computer Assisted Language Learning* (CALL) described by Warschauer (1996) in his popular historical account, *concordancing* can be seen to shift the computer assisted language learning paradigm from a process-control model to an information-resource model, allowing learners to explore language for themselves while the instructor's role becomes one of simply providing the tools and resources (Cobb 1997). Some researchers claim that this provides the basis for inductive language learning by students as they investigate the evidence from searches for words and phrases to discover or confirm patterns of usage and the ways meaning is constructed by their use (Todd 2001; Johns 1986; Johns 1991).

When a corpus or body of texts is collected and stored on a computer or network, a *concordancing* program allows users to search for a word or phrase and produce an output, either on screen or in print, which lists all occurrences of the searched words, showing lines of text in which those words appear. The output can show whole sentences, or only limited sections of text surrounding the searched word or phrase, depending on the settings chosen by the user. Figure 1 shows a basic concordance for the word *different* found when searching a corpus of agricultural science texts.

From such an output, students might infer that a plural noun group usually follows the word *different* unless it is preceded by the indefinite article, in which case a singular noun follows it. Lines 8 and 9 demonstrate this clearly and other lines demonstrate uses of the word *different* with the definite article, in complex noun groups (*different ecophysiological tolerances*) and with the verb 'to be' (*is very different to*). This set of results could be used in a classroom to demonstrate several aspects of the use of the word in a sentence. When looking at examples of use in complex noun groups from texts within

No.	Concordance line
1	to increase extractable P concentrations in ***different*** soil types that are used for dairy pasture pr
2	ffect of P fertiliser form on ÆEP values for ***different*** soils is also not known. There is an increasi
3	nt study, we determined the ÆEP values for 9 ***different*** pasture soils, 6 and 12 months after P fertilizer
4	ying concentrations of P as KH2PO4 to give 9 ***different*** initial P concentrations ranging from 0 to 80
5	similar amounts of P fertiliser resulted in ***different*** ÆEP values at each of the 9 sites. The ÆEPOls
6	measured from the 0-10 cm layer. The use of ***different*** samples from the upper layer of the soil could
7	.) A.J. Scott, a species normally found in a ***different*** environment at higher elevations of Mediterra
8	n under study and two others were taken from ***different*** tussocks in a neighbouring lagoon with impede
9	hybrid were taken, each from the centre of a ***different*** tussock from which S. perennis had also been
10	5 Depth profiles of below-ground dry mass in ***different*** vegetational zones of tussocks in the well-dr
11	have been several hybridization events with ***different*** pollen parents (Ayres & Strong 2001). The Sa
12	ssocks) that each individual resulted from a ***different*** pollination. Despite the dominant effects of
13	en reciprocal (Anttila et al. 2000) and nine ***different*** categories of hybrid, indicating backcrossing
14	in a Mediterranean salt marsh determined by ***different*** ecophysiological tolerances. Journal of Ecolo
15	curve for 14CO2 samples was determined using ***different*** quantities of 1 M NaOH and counts were corre
16	terms of the amounts recovered in each of the ***different*** pools (i.e. microbial, soil, respired, and pl
17	t is in direct contact with the soil is very ***different*** to patterns of herbicide degradation when it
18	sulfuron and metsulfuron-methyl in soils from ***different*** depths. Weed Research 29, 281-287. Wardle, D
19	e vegetation index (NDVI) was tested in five ***different*** ecosystems and significant correlations were
20	e used to test the robustness of the MSDI in ***different*** biomes. We established fence-line contrasts a
21	ds to changes in the distribution pattern of ***different*** types of vegetation cover, and not necessaril
22	of arid and semi-arid ecosystems of markedly ***different*** vegetation structure. Using this approach, it

Figure 1. KWIC (key word in context) concordance output from a search for *different*

their discipline of study, students can see examples from within the texts related to the discipline in which they are writing.

Most *concordancing* programs also have other functions, such as word frequency tests. A frequency test produces a list of all words that appear in all of the texts in the corpus, showing how many unique words and total words make up the texts. The list can then be sorted by frequency and can be used as a starting point for discourse analysis. Such a test of a collection of texts related to the Computer Assisted Language Learning course taught in the Discipline of Linguistics at the University of Adelaide in 2004 produced a list of 8,347 unique words. While the total number of words used in the

Unique words = 8437   Total words = 66278

1	The	3709	5.5961 %	32	from	208	0.3138 %
2	of	2477	3.7373 %	33	new	191	0.2882 %
3	and	2258	3.4069 %	34	student	185	0.2791 %
4	to	1555	2.3462 %	35	more	183	0.2761 %
5	in	1359	2.0505 %	36	teaching	182	0.2746 %
6	A	1097	1.6551 %	37	have	181	0.2731 %
7	for	670	1.0109 %	38	classroom	180	0.2716 %
8	on	576	0.8691 %	39	research	178	0.2686 %
9	Learning	564	0.8510 %	40	was	176	0.2655 %
10	is	553	0.8344 %	41	Information	171	0.2580 %
11	that	518	0.7816 %	42	they	166	0.2505 %
12	as	506	0.7635 %	43	computer	165	0.2490 %
13	students	456	0.6880 %	44	which	165	0.2490 %
14	with	410	0.6186 %	45	University	159	0.2399 %
15	are	364	0.5492 %	46	educational	147	0.2218 %
16	technology	344	0.5190 %	47	Internet	147	0.2218 %
17	or	325	0.4904 %	48	Other	147	0.2218 %
18	be	302	0.4557 %	49	resources	140	0.2112 %
19	this	272	0.4104 %	50	also	134	0.2022 %
20	at	255	0.3847 %	51	teachers	134	0.2022 %
21	An	251	0.3787 %	52	course	131	0.1977 %
22	online	250	0.3772 %	53	teacher	128	0.1931 %
23	by	243	0.3666 %	54	m	126	0.1901 %
24	education	239	0.3606 %	55	one	124	0.1871 %
25	use	232	0.3500 %	56	these	123	0.1856 %
26	Language	231	0.3485 %	57	s	118	0.1780 %
27	their	229	0.3455 %	58	P	117	0.1765 %
28	Web	228	0.3440 %	59	Communication	115	0.1735 %
29	it	224	0.3380 %	60	using	115	0.1735 %
30	not	210	0.3168 %	61	computers	110	0.1660 %
31	were	210	0.3168 %	62	some	110	0.1660 %

Figure 2. Frequency list of a CALL corpus, showing the first 62 words only.

texts was 66,278, this total arose from many of the so-called unique words being used more than once. For example, *the* is used 3,709 times and *technology* is used 344 times, giving a combined total of 4,053 words for only two unique words, *the* and *technology*. The first 62 unique words shown in Figure 2 show something of the nature of the discourses within the texts, and examinations of similar lists from other corpora highlight the ways in which the different texts work: the kinds of content words and grammatical words used most frequently, the kinds of actions and relationships that are apparent in verbs and the subject matter that is apparent in the nouns.

Another common feature of *concordancing* software is the availability of a frequency list for collocates after a word search. Figure 2 shows the 52 most common left collocates for the word *learning* in a combined corpus, sorted by frequency. Most of the texts in which the word was found originally came from a linguistics

Left collocates for [learning | = 152

1	Language	76	27	when	5
2	and	66	28	as	4
3	of	43	29	Emotions	4
4	the	40	30	independent	4
5	based	20	31	influence	4
6	for	19	32	mediated	4
7	student	19	33	open	4
8	on	17	34	that	4
9	Online	17	35	with	4
10	Teaching	16	36	Affective	3
11	collaborative	15	37	classroom	3
12	to	15	38	Distributed	3
13	assisted	14	39	improved	3
14	in	13	40	literacy	3
15	their	12	41	self	3
16	distance	11	42	Attitude	2
17	a	8	43	authentic	2
18	active	7	44	behavioral	2
19	cooperative	6	45	constructivist	2
20	further	6	46	Education	2
21	s	6	47	electronic	2
22	Asynchronous	5	48	ESL	2
23	cognitive	5	49	individual	2
24	Higher	5	50	Integrated	2
25	students	5	51	Interactive	2
26	supported	5	52	lifelong	2

Figure 3. Word frequency list for left collocates of learning in a combined corpus.

corpus and were therefore related to language learning. The frequency of collocations can demonstrate similar features of texts in other disciplines and in different genres, depending on how the texts are initially sorted into their respective corpora.

This latter point demonstrates the need to apply some care when selecting texts for a corpus. The purpose of the corpus must be clear at the outset because one comprised of texts from a limited set, perhaps in the style of only one or two writers, will be limited in its ability to demonstrate a range of examples of usage. A range of writers within a field makes for a more practical corpus when models of language usage are being sought. Similarly, thought must be given to the range of subject matter represented in the texts, or the features demonstrated by the texts may not be exactly those intended. For example, a student studying the frequency list in Figure 3 may erroneously assume that *language* is the most common left collocate of *learning* in English, when in fact the result is skewed due to the nature of the texts included in the corpus used. The work of David Lee (Lee 2001) on corpus samples developed for the British National Corpus Sampler gives some insight into the complex tasks of selecting and sorting texts for use in corpora that are intended to demonstrate examples of usage across a range of subject areas and across a range of writers.

Another important consideration is one of the software that learners are going to use to search their corpora. Software in this field is not usually designed for language learners to use: it is typically designed for language researchers and is often complex to operate. It also uses jargon familiar only to linguists and language specialists, adding to the time and effort necessary for students and teachers to learn. *ConcApp* (Greaves 1996) was selected for the initial trials at the University of Adelaide because it was suitable for use with the multiple corpora containing texts of various disciplines, it was easy for students to learn how to use and it was free. Web-based concordancers often have limitations and do not focus on the various academic disciplines required. They typically process only small texts which must be pasted into a text window, or they will only search the sample texts provided as a corpus on the host web site. These would not have been suitable for the purposes of the initial research, but one web concordancer (Greaves 1998) did prove useful for students when words could not be found in the academic corpora developed especially for the project. In a later trial at Flinders University, students found that many of their questions about structuring sentences around words that they were learning to use could be answered by searching the corpora provided on this website (Adams 2006).

Some of the commercially available software is packaged with sample corpora, and some sample corpora can be bought and downloaded from the Internet, but none suited the purposes of the initial discipline-specific language investigation. The need for discipline-specific corpora across several disciplines led to the development of an entirely new set of corpora, a development which is continuing. Legal advice was sought in regard to the use of published and copyrighted texts for the corpora, which were intended to be freely available to students and also had to be of professional quality. The corpora were therefore composed of material held or subscribed to by the University's library, or contributed by academics if they held the copyright on the texts. Corpora developed in this way could only be made available to staff and students at the University of Adelaide, a possible limiting factor in future cases where corpora are to be made more widely available.

The research being referred to here can be broadly described as having taken place in four stages. Firstly, applied linguistics postgraduates at the University of Adelaide were exposed to the *ConcApp* program and small trial corpora in an introductory session to stimulate discussion and to gather ideas for future stages of the research. Secondly, international agricultural science postgraduates and researchers were introduced to *ConcApp* and expanded trial corpora. The third and most extensive stage involved exposing international students from the University of Adelaide's Pre-enrolment English Program (PEP) to *ConcApp* and a range of corpora from several disciplines, as well as some non-academic corpora. In the final stage, international postgraduate students of public administration at Flinders University were introduced to the Web Concordancer and its online corpora.

The purpose of the research was to trial the *concordancing* approach in both discipline specific and general academic contexts, as well as compare the use of *concordancing* software and in-house corpora with the use of a web-based approach using online corpora. The trials also allowed comparisons between a simple introduction and the ongoing, supported learning of *concordancing* as an integrated part of daily classroom practice. Students in the PEP were able to experience the *concordancing* approach as a part of their classroom activities over a period of ten weeks with help and encouragement from a teacher, whereas all other groups were simply introduced to the process in a single session of 45 minutes.

As the corpora were expanded throughout the first three stages of the research project, it allowed for an increasing focus on demonstrable differences between text types, and an increasing focus by students on their need to learn the idiomatic expressions that were regular features of the texts of their disciplines of study. The linguistics students showed interest in using the *ConcApp* program to research language but the agricultural science students showed more interest in using it as a tool to improve their writing skills, some wanting to develop their own corpora The most extensive stage involved PEP students, who were a mix of undergraduate and postgraduate students, and their needs appeared to be for guidance in the more general aspects of grammar and usage. While they had access to a more elaborate collection of discipline-specific corpora than the earlier groups, they favoured the use of a mixed corpus of academic texts and also found the Web Concordancer useful when words could not be found using *ConcApp* (Adams 2006). It was this outcome that led to the trial of the Web Concordancer in the later stage.

At the end of the four stages of the study, results suggested that several factors contribute to a student's interest in and continued use of *concordancing*. These factors include the manner in which *concordancing* is introduced and the facilities used, with a step-by-step demonstration projected on a screen being more effective than students being directed while they use it on their own computers.

A further factor relates to the timing of an introduction in relation to a student's writing load. Students involved in thesis writing were more positive, and more likely to express interest in developing their own corpora for *ConcApp*, while undergraduate students found that the web-based concordancer or a more general corpus for use with *ConcApp* was suitable for their needs.

Ongoing support and personal encouragement from a teacher familiar with *concordancing* practice in the classroom was also a significant factor in the long-term uptake of the approach. Students who were simply introduced to *concordancing* and left to use it independently for several months, usually gave up. Even those students who were involved in postgraduate research and who had initially expressed interest in developing their own corpora were not using the software when surveyed eight months later (Cargill & Adams 2005). On the other hand, undergraduates with little pressure to produce written work but who had regularly used the software for several weeks in a classroom were, in most cases, still using it almost one year later and still saw it as a valuable contribution to learning the correct use of words and phrases in their writing (Adams 2006).

Further confirmation of the value of *concordancing* as a tool for developing high level writing skills has implications for teachers and organisations involved in the teaching of these skills to ELL students. As a result of the various stages of this research, *concordancing* has been adopted as an approach to writing development within the Graduate

Centre at the University of Adelaide, and by some teachers within the PEP at the University of Adelaide. Following early successes in these environments, it is also being introduced to students at Flinders University through consultations and teaching sessions at the Student Learning Centre.

The different responses of teachers to the *concordancing* approach raise issues that require our attention. Some have greeted the approach enthusiastically as a refreshing approach to improving language usage; some have been suspicious and quick to object, preferring to continue with practices which are more familiar. The research referred to here seems to have identified teacher support and therefore teacher cooperation as an important issue (Adams 2006).

Other important questions also remain open to future research. Although this study and others have so far focused on the use of *concordancing* in universities, there is also scope for similar study into its use in other contexts. Mention has been made of the possibility of the approach being used in programs aimed at migrant professionals, but scope for use with school students should not be ignored. This is, after all, where professional writing skills begin to grow.

References

Adams, R 2006, Factors affecting student use of concordancing: comparisons of instructional methodology, MA thesis, Centre for European Studies and General Linguistics, University of Adelaide, Adelaide.

Cargill, M. & Adams R 2005, 'Learning discipline-specific research English for a world stage: a self-access concordancing tool' in *Higher Education in a Changing World: 2005 HERDSA Annual Conference*, Higher Education Research and Development Society of Australia, Sydney.

Cobb, T 1997, Is there any measurable learning from hands-on concordancing? *System*, vol. 25, no. 3, pp. 301–315.

Craswell, G 1992, 'International Graduate Coursework Students and the Urgency of Adapting to New Learning Strategies', Technical Report/Occasional Paper no. GS92/2, Graduate School, Australian National University, Canberra.

Gledhill, C 1999b, 'The phraseology of rhetoric, collocations and discourse in cancer research abstracts' in *'Knowledge and Discourse' International Multidisciplinary Conference*, University of Hong Kong, Hong Kong.

Gledhill, C 2000, 'The discourse function of collocation in research article introductions'. in *English for Specific Purposes*, vol. 19, pp. 151–135, viewed 17 August 2003 <www.elsevier.com/locate/esp>

Greaves, C 1996, *ConcApp*. Edict Virtual Language Centre, Hong Kong.

Greaves, C 1998, *Web Concordancer*. Hong Kong Polytechnic University. viewed 12 April 2006, <http://vlc.polyu.edu.hk/concordance/WWWConcappE.htm>

Johns, T 1986, 'Micro-concord: a language learner's resource tool' in *System*,vol.14, no. 2, pp. 151–162.

Johns, T 1991, 'Should you be persuaded – two samples of data-driven learning materials' in *English Language Research Journal*, vol. pp. 1–16.

Johns, T 1994, 'From printout to handout: grammar and vocabulary teaching in the context of data-driven learning' in *Approaches to Pedagogic Grammar*, ed T. Odlin, Cambridge University Press, Cambridge, UK.

Koyama, Y, Nakano, T & Matsuura, C 2003, 'Development of an ESP E-Learning Tool Using In-House Corpora' in *Knowledge-based Information and Engineering Systems, 7th International Conference, KES 2003.*, 533–539, Springer, Oxford.

Lee, D. 2001, 'Genres, Registers, Text Types, Domains and Styles: Clarifying the Concepts and Navigating a Path Through the BNC Jungle' in *Language Learning and Technology*, vol. 5, no. 3, pp. 37–72, viewed 24 March 2006 <http://llt.msu.edu/vol5num3/lee/default.html>

Lee, D & Swales, J 2006, 'A corpus-based EAP course for NNS doctoral students: Moving from available specialized corpora to self-compiled corpora' in *English for Specific Purposes*, vol. 25, no. 56–75.

Lewis, M 1994, *The Lexical Approach*, Language Teaching Publications, London.

Nelson, M 2003, 'Worldly Experience' in *Guardian Weekly*, 20 March 2003.

Sawir, E 2005, 'Language difficulties of international students in Australia: The effects of prior learning experience' in *International Education Journal*, vol. 6, no. 5, pp. 567–580.

Stevens, V 1995, 'Concordancing with Language Learners: Why? When? What?' in *CAELL Journal*, vol. 6, no. 2, pp. 2–10.

Swales, JM & Feak, C 2000, *English in today's research world: a writing guide*, University of Michigan Press, Ann Arbor.

Thurstun, J & Candlin, C 1998, 'Concordancing and the teaching of the vocabulary of academic English' in *English for Specific Purposes*, vol. 17, no. 3, pp. 267–280.

Todd, RW 2001, 'Induction from self-selected concordances and self-correction' in *System*, vol. 29, no.1, pp. 91–102.

Tribble, C 1989, 'The use of text structuring vocabulary in native and non-native speaker writing' in *MUESLI News*, June 1989, pp. 17–20.

Warschauer, M 1996, 'Computer-assisted language learning: An introduction' in *Multimedia Language Teaching*, ed S. Fotos, Logos International, Tokyo, pp. 3–20.

Developing local content material for a New-Arrivals program

Glenda Inverarity

The overall aims of *Certificate III in Spoken and Written English* in Australia are to assist newly-arrived migrants 'undertake further education and training, seek and maintain employment, and participate in the community' (Adult Migrant English Program 1992, p. 5). When students first attend classes, settlement needs are a high priority, in addition to improving their English. Settlement needs include issues such as health and wellbeing, shopping and banking, work and study, personal and social interactions, orientation and transport, and accommodation.

This chapter discusses the process of developing a content-based instructional package to assist students new to the country understand the Adelaide rental property market. Student issues to be taken into account are identified before the first development and use of the materials is described, followed by reflections on successes and failures. Then, using these insights, the materials are amended and described in their draft two form. Finally, after using draft two with students, further reflections are discussed regarding plans for draft three. The purpose is to demonstrate to the reader how reflective thinking can assist in the development of content-based learning material.

Student issues

The needs of *New-Arrivals* vary according to their country of origin, visa type, and the length of time since their arrival. For example, country of origin can affect how a person manages to negotiate a city. Many *New-Arrivals* come from small villages and rural settings or refugee camps, and have no experience using public transport, or reading a city map or street directory.

Students' visa type will also have various influences on their settlement. For example, in a class where students were discussing rental accommodation, one Asian student—the spouse of a wealthy business migrant—divulged her large weekly rent, which was more than most of the students received for their entire weekly Centrelink allowance. Visa type also influences the help *New-Arrivals* receive. For example, refugees often receive assistance from service agencies with finding permanent accommodation; however, people with temporary protection visas must manage this task without agency support or assistance.

The length of time students have been in the country is an issue that impacts on the development of the learning materials. Some students, usually mothers with school-age children, cannot attend classes immediately, as their children are not allowed to start school until the family is in permanent accommodation. This is because the Education Department believes it is too disruptive when children have to change schools after only a few weeks or months. Hence, the mother has often been in Australia for about three months and has already found a permanent place to live. Therefore, the learning materials need to be engaging enough to hold the attention of those who have already met this settlement need.

Continual class intakes are another important factor to be considered. It is not unusual to be halfway through the term with twelve or so students reasonably well settled when new students arrive. They may also need to find permanent accommodation, but will have missed this unit of work. Students in this situation are provided with copies of all handouts, which allow them to see what they have missed, and work through those materials. These handouts are also important because all students are expected to achieve the same learning outcomes. Problems regarding this handout policy are identified in the development of draft one of the materials.

First development and use of materials

This interesting journey began during the first week of term when a student asked the lecturer to explain how to find a rental property. Over a ten week term lecturers are required to test five learning outcomes, so it was inappropriate to spend more than two weeks (about eighteen hours) on this topic.

Rental accommodation advertisements from Saturday's local newspaper, *The Advertiser*, formed the basis of the learning materials.

The first point of study was decoding the abbreviations. A worksheet was developed to help students explore and decode the myriad of abbreviations landlords devise to keep their advertising costs to a minimum. The advertisements contained no systematic use of regular abbreviations.

The abbreviations were painstakingly decoded: some the students were able to guess, but for others the skills required were beyond their vocabulary and local knowledge. For example, the various abbreviations used for 'bedroom' could usually be identified, but others were more obscure such as 'gge umr', meaning that the garage is under the main roof of the house.

The next information that required decoding concerned the various accommodation types—in other words, the difference between an executive townhouse, a townhouse, a unit, a flat, a row house, and a heritage cottage. A walk to a nearby inner suburb that had an eclectic mix of old and new, cottage and mansion properties helped put housing types into perspective.

Students then had to find three accommodation advertisements of interest, decode and rework them. A crossword puzzle using abbreviation features from the advertisements was included. Looking at the map of Adelaide, students identified some of the suburbs from the newspaper.

For the final activity, students were to list advertisements that showed both the suburb and weekly rental price, calculate the average rental costs by suburb, and enter the averages onto a worksheet. Each student was given one column of advertisements from which they were to list suburbs and prices. Explicit instructions were given and demonstrated. This was a homework exercise; some students completed the homework but others did not. Using these lists, students were instructed to calculate the average rents; some students knew how to do this but others did not. With the lecturer's assistance, average rents for about thirty suburbs were calculated. This was seen as an important numeracy activity.

As an exercise driven by *authentic* newspaper texts and lecturer explanation, the fundamental question of how to find a rental property was answered. However, it was found that when new students entered the course a few weeks late, the handouts provided to the new students lacked meaning.

Description of draft one

Draft one of the learning materials included six photocopied pages from the newspaper, reduced from A3 to A4 size. On the first page was the newspaper index, and on the next five, advertisements from the newspaper's Accommodation section. All six pages were without explanation of the material they contained, so students arriving late to the course had no guidance as to what they should focus their attention on.

The seventh page contained a list of abbreviations for students to guess. When developing draft one, the lecturer sat with students and explained each abbreviation, so students were able to decode the terms reasonably successfully. However, when new students arrived later in the term, it was realised that without lecturer assistance they would be unable to decode many meanings. Therefore, they received the answer key as page eight.

On pages nine and ten was the exercise where students selected, recorded and decoded three housing advertisements of interest. The crossword puzzle followed, along with a reduced map of Adelaide suburbs, and an index. Although the map was small, it did allow students to locate suburbs, so it served its basic purpose. The fourteenth page included a table listing 145 suburbs where accommodation was available. The table was labelled 'Average rental prices in Adelaide by suburb'. There were no average prices in the columns alongside the suburbs, calculating this was a whole class exercise; because it would be a near impossible task for an individual student.

Successes and failures

There were some obvious reflections regarding successes and failures of draft one. Firstly, the print size was inappropriate after pages from the newspaper were reduced. Secondly, there was a complete lack of instructions to guide students through the document. Decoding abbreviations was a worthwhile exercise, but without the answer key it was too difficult. This problem had been anticipated, and draft one did provide the answer key for students who joined the course late. However, in reflection, students who had completed the exercise in class may have been disempowered because there were many abbreviations unknown to them, and the exercise was extremely lecturer driven. Therefore, it was decided in future to provide students with the answer key to empower them to decode the advertisements independently.

Calculating the average rent for suburbs was considered too large a task and overwhelmed many of the students. However, one success did eventuate: a student who had permanent accommodation calculated the average rent for the suburb in which she was living, and discovered she was paying a lot more than average. She decided that when her current lease expired she would look for better value, and felt she had better knowledge of what to look for next time. Thus, it was decided to limit the average rent calculations to one suburb, and that way students could focus on the suburb where they lived.

The walk to the inner suburb was pleasant, but not the most purposeful use of an excursion. Conversely, the photographs that were taken during the walk could be used to create a visual reference bank, to be accessed during computing lessons in a format that even a beginner could use. This resource could be linked to a worksheet to make a meaningful exercise.

An additional concern was that the materials were not meaningful enough to engage students who had already found suitable accommodation. Feez (2002, p. 108) makes this point when she states: 'A topic is used to unify a set of contexts of use, syllabus elements and language learning activities.'

The final consideration was to question the language goals of the whole exercise, and wonder whether students could achieve a learning outcome upon completion of the unit of work. Abbreviations are one obvious language feature, as are the local ways of writing addresses, so it was thought that completing personal information forms could be incorporated into the materials as a learning outcome (the learner can complete a formatted text).

Second development of materials

In draft one, a photocopy of the newspaper's index was included, however, the reader was not provided with any explanation as to why the index was there. New students, not realising its purpose, may have mistakenly thought they were meant to read the article about the Pie

Cart instead, which also featured on the page. Certainly no context was assumable, which meant the handout was fairly meaningless.

The first change to the material was to consider it a self-study unit of work that could also be lecturer driven in the first instance in the classroom. The materials need to be self-explanatory in self-studies. As Dickinson (1994, p. 80) explains, in constructing learning materials we 'need to keep in mind that when they are in use there may be no readily available lecturer to administer, supplement or explain them. Consequently, the materials themselves should ideally contain the help and information which a lecturer would supply.' This was the starting point for draft two of the 'Renting in Adelaide' materials.

Description of draft two

In draft two, a cover page has been designed to inform students what the unit of work is about: 'Renting in Adelaide'. This page also advises students what they will need in order to complete the unit of work: a copy of *The Advertiser*, scissors and glue, a calculator, a map of Adelaide, a pen and a ruler for graphing. They would also need to work with another class member for discussions and surveys. Objectives and learning outcomes are also described.

The second page contains the newspaper index found in draft one, but now includes information about the material's relevance. Students are informed that the index is on page two of *The Advertiser*, and accommodation is listed in the Classified section. There is an arrow pointing to the relevant part of the index.

The third page has explanations for each of the sub-headings in the Accommodation section: Houses to Let, Serviced Apartments, Rooms to Let, and Share Accommodation. Students are then required to answer some guided questions: How many people will they be living with? Do they want the responsibility of looking after a large garden? Would they be prepared to live in a small flat? Students are asked to consider their responses before thinking about their own special needs and asking classmates about what is important to them. The materials now include some 'getting to know you' speaking activities.

The fourth page has a list of abbreviations and their meanings, so that students do not need to guess the answers, nor does it fall upon the lecturer to explain them. Students will become familiar with the terms by decoding the enlarged advertisements on the next page.

Selected advertisements from the Share Accommodation section have been included for reading. This is important because some of the single men do consider this option. Sharing accommodation can be difficult, so a short newspaper article about the topic and a list of things you should know before agreeing to share follows this page. There is reference to a web address with information about sharing, and students are instructed to write some notes from the web page. Class interaction is again encouraged, because students must write questions they could ask people they may want to share with, and try them out in the classroom. This builds more 'getting to know you' activities into the early stages of the course, as an *authentic* spoken activity.

Page nine explains how to write addresses in Australia, and includes information about common abbreviations for titles. This serves as an introduction to filling in forms—one of the learning outcomes students are to achieve during one term. Students are provided with an explanation about Australian postcodes and where to find them, and are encouraged to search for an Internet site where postcode information can be found, for future reference. Students are to practise writing different addresses using advertisements from the Accommodation section.

In draft two, information about phone numbers, the codes for international calls to Australia, and the Adelaide area code is supplied. This was information that previous students did not know when undertaking the task of filling in forms. To practise this skill, students complete the personal details section of two forms, the second of which is the Medicare document used to advise change of address; so this exercise has direct benefits for students when they do find permanent accommodation. Students will be encouraged to brainstorm who they would need to advise of a change of address, and computing time could be spent drafting a letter to inform these people/organisations.

Students then return to searching for accommodation, and this time they need to find advertisements for a suburb they would like to live in. They are to cut and paste the advertisements onto the page before calculating the average rent for that suburb. Students are to survey seven other class members to collect data about a total of eight suburbs with average rents and then draw a graph to visually represent the information collected in their survey. This exercise has been introduced because numeracy skills are to be included in the *curriculum*, and graphing is often difficult for students. This section will probably require some lecturer guidance, and could be carried into computing activities where students create graphs in *Excel*. Two required learning outcomes of *Certificate III* are to be able to read and write graphs, so this serves as a brief introduction to work the students will undertake in second term.

Using full size maps of Adelaide, students are to locate the eight suburbs they recorded average rents for, and discuss these with the class. Then, students need to write and practise a discussion with a landlord to obtain information about an advertised rental property. This is where students who have already found accommodation will be able to tell other students, via role play, about their own experiences of speaking with landlords.

Finally, draft two includes information about the rights and responsibilities of tenants and landlords. A web address is supplied where students can view a basic rental agreement and become familiar with the contents, before a landlord presents them with one to sign.

Omissions

For several reasons, it has been decided not to include the walk to the inner suburb to examine housing types. Firstly, it is impractical to always go for a walk due to weather and time constraints. Secondly, the inner suburb is not at all representative of the suburbs students will be renting in. Therefore, digital photographs will be taken of housing types typical to suburbs where students live, and these will be entered into a multimedia program to be accessed during computing time. An inadvertent omission of draft two is the vocabulary used in the legal jargon about rights and responsibilities and lease agreements. This could also be addressed in draft three.

Reflective thinking

Drafting and re-drafting a unit of work requires much reflective thinking, and as Farrell (2004, p. 11) states, 'effective reflective practitioners go a step beyond simply acknowledging successes and failures in the classroom [,] by striving to figure out why some topics or approaches worked and others did not'. He suggests that lecturers reflect on their tendencies. The lecturer in this study has a tendency towards developing work that is lecturer-driven. For example, decoding the abbreviations worked effectively as a class exercise: students were engaged in listening and writing the meanings. However, with so many abbreviations unknown to them, students were disempowered by the exercise, because it relied heavily on lecturer explanation.

Testing of draft two

Draft two was given to a new group of students and, as anticipated, having the full forms of the abbreviations did empower them to decode the advertisements. They struggled with writing addresses, proving this was something they needed to learn. The section on share accommodation was skipped because it was not relevant to this group. Furthermore, on reflection, this section is not relevant to the vast majority of students in the Adult Migrant English Program, so this section will probably be deleted in the third draft.

The students had difficulty following the instructions to cut and paste advertisements for a suburb that they would like to live in; therefore, this section will be re-written as a sequential procedural text. Being able to read and follow procedural texts is a learning outcome students will need to achieve during the term, so it will be a good opportunity to give them early exposure and practice.

As students were working on this section it also became apparent that they did not always understand that the name of the suburb was the first word of the advertisement, therefore a page containing this explanation is to be inserted early in the materials.

Overview

There were several positive outcomes from this section of work. Firstly, students were encouraged to buy the Saturday *Advertiser* and use it in this exercise. As Sanderson (1999, p. 3) states, 'newspapers are an invaluable source of authentic materials, and their use in the language classroom is very much in keeping with current thinking and practice in teaching pedagogy'. In this case, students were given an opportunity to work with materials to assist their settlement.

In their discussion of EFL, Cortazzi and Jin (1999, p. 197) identify three broad *aims*, one of which is 'the development of communicative competence for use in situations the learner might expect to encounter'. This is even more important in teaching settlement skills, and this unit of work addresses a definite settlement need of students: it equips them to negotiate their way towards finding suitable, permanent accommodation.

Secondly, one student found an advertisement he thought was good and asked if he could phone the number. The lecturer explained that the newspaper used in the exercise was a few weeks old, and that the house would no longer be available. The student immediately said that he should get the paper next Saturday and phone if there is a suitable advertisement. For this student the learning materials had been meaningful.

Overall, this unit of work represents a unique and worthwhile exercise. It assists settlement, works towards learning outcomes, includes 'getting to know you' speaking exercises, uses *authentic* texts, and is relevant to the local environment. Further study is needed to evaluate the usefulness of local content for the range of students in adult migrant classes.

References

Adult Migrant English Program 1992, *Certificate III in Spoken and Written English,* 4th edn, Department of Education and Training, Sydney.

Cortazzi, M & Jin, L 1999, 'Cultural mirrors: Materials and methods in the EFL classroom' in *Culture in Second Language Teaching and Learning,* ed E Hinkel, Cambridge University Press, Cambridge, pp. 196–219.

Dickinson, L 1994, *Self-instruction in Language Learning,* Cambridge University Press, Cambridge.

Farrell, TSC 2004, *Reflective Practice in Action: 80 Reflection Breaks for Busy Teachers,* Corwin Press, California.

Feez, S 2002, *Text-based Syllabus Design,* Adult Multicultural Education Service, Sydney.

Sanderson, P 1999, *Using Newspapers in the Classroom,* Cambridge University Press, Cambridge.

Aboriginal patients and non-Aboriginal health professionals' discourse—some issues to consider

Fiona Ryan

Effective communication between Aboriginal patients from remote communities and non-Aboriginal health professionals is an important issue affecting service delivery, patient satisfaction and health outcomes.

Research aimed specifically at analysing communication between health professionals and Aboriginal patients is limited to a few studies in the Northern Territory (Edis 1985; Cass, A, Lowell, A, Christie, M, Snelling, PL, Flack, M, Marrnganyin, B & Brown, I 2002). However, in the broader field of Aboriginal health research, a number of issues related to communication have been identified and will be discussed in this paper:

- The discrepancy of the western style question-and-answer sequence used commonly by non-indigenous health professionals when communicating with Aboriginal patients whose L1 was not English.
- The differences in world views relating to health and illness held by many Aboriginal people.
- The different communication cues that Aboriginal patients and non-Aboriginal health professionals use and respond to in communication.

Communication is recognised by both Aboriginal people and non-Aboriginal people as a barrier to effective delivery of health services. *The South Australian Department of Human Services Final Report of the Generational Health Review* (2003, p. 20) states that:

> Participation is important for quality of life, health and wellbeing, and is an important mechanism for service improvement and quality and safety. In all businesses, talking to one's customers is one of the basic principles of operation. It is no different for health.

It further states that 'Issues of miscommunication in the provision of health services to Aboriginal people are significant' (p. 109). Ong, LML, DeHaes JCJM, Hoos AM & Lammes, FB (1995) state that 'to ultimately improve longer-term patient outcomes, such as quality of life, health, status, symptom resolution or survival, research should identify communicative behaviours and interactions that produce these desired outcomes'(p. 914).

The question-and-answer style of communication

The discourse between Aboriginal patients and non-Aboriginal health care professionals is based on the discourse rules and structures of the institutions in which the communication takes place. Research shows several things. Firstly, that where one communicative form predominates, such as the form of question-and-answer exchanges, communicative expectations of health professionals are often different from the communicative expectations of Aboriginal patients (Devitt & McMasters 1998a). Secondly, that communication barriers can prevent health service providers from being able to diagnose patients' complaints using the question-and-answer form. This leads to problems such as insufficient information being given to Aboriginal patients about their condition, misunderstandings about consent for medical procedures, insufficient health education and health problems prevention information being given to Aboriginal patients, and difficulties faced by medical practitioners in accurately diagnosing health problems (Trudgen 2000). Research shows that western modes of discourse dominate, often to the exclusion of Aboriginal modes of communication, which can impact on clinical management of the patient (Cass et al. 2002).

Eades (1982), in a linguistic study of information seeking in an Aboriginal cultural context in South East Queensland (not however in the health context), found that when she asked Aboriginal people direct questions, they often were 'confused, dysfluent or non-compliant' (p. 65). However, the use of a declarative as a question, with a question intonation, was answered without a problem. Her study showed that within that particular Aboriginal culture, seeking information through speech can be fulfilled directly by asking questions or indirectly by making a provocative statement' (p. 66), such as by presenting information for confirmation.

Harkins (1995) proposes that Aboriginal speakers of English in the Alice Springs area may also operate according to an Aboriginal economy of information when they use English and in their lack of questioning of others. This stems from Aboriginal cultural constraints, which see knowledge as given when certain others, such as elders, see it as appropriate to give information, rather than assuming the right to ask for it.

Eades'(1982) study upholds this view, finding that the transmission of information in the community she studied was socially mediated by:

- constraints on who has legitimate access to particular information
- the person requiring information having to wait until the knowledgeable person decided whether and when to give the information
- information exchange being based on relationships between speakers and discourse protocols such as '… the person requiring information must present some known, inferred or guessed information, in an appropriate mode. When and if the knowledgeable person decides to, he then presents his information' (Eades 1982, p. 72).

There are historical examples of communication that show that Aboriginal people did not recognise the question-and-answer format. Malcolm and Koscielecki (1997, p. 51), in a report to the Australian Research Council on Aboriginal English, show that 'Aboriginal people did not recognise the same *pragmatic* force in requests for information or services that the Europeans saw in them.' Malcolm and Koscielecki's historical review makes reference to other authors regarding questioning where Aboriginal people might not respond (Dawson 1987, pp. 228 - 229; Millett 1980, p. 298; Hassell 1975, p. 58), where they might give an abstract look (Telfer 1939, p. 85), or 'feign ignorance of the matter about which information was being sought' (Dawson 1987, p. 303). The historical review also found that requests may have been responded to with minimal response after some delay (Troy 1990, p. 130). Settlers noted failure to express gratitude and evaluated this negatively (von Hugel & Baron 1994, p. 420). Barley (1984, p. 29) stated that 'Reciprocity and sharing were fundamental to their way of life to such an extent that their language contained no word for "thank-you"'. Malcolm and Koscielecki (1997, p. 52) state:

> The retention of the pragmatics of requesting and thanking, whereby requests do not require mitigation and services do not require thanks, was linked to the retention of the view of mutual obligation associated with the traditional Aboriginal life.

They suggest that these historical *pragmatic* contrasts have been maintained in many respects to the present day, and Aboriginal people have adopted an English-based form of communication in the context of the continuity of their cultural identification as Aboriginal people.

Further communication factors

Edis (1998) recorded simulated interviews between non-Aboriginal health professionals and Aboriginal Yolngu clients, from remote communities in the Northern Territory, presenting with a variety of medical problems. She points out a number of factors that contributed to miscommunication in the simulations—patient responses not always matching health professionals' questions; direct questions receiving unconvincing 'yes' answers; Aboriginal participants remaining silent for long periods following a question; comments being cut off or finished by the other partner; particular words being misunderstood by either party; and inconsistencies of the clients from one response or statement to another. Medical terms were sometimes misinterpreted by Aboriginal participants and descriptions of symptoms given by medical practitioners differed from descriptions by Aboriginal participants.

Concepts of quantity, distance, time (duration, onset and frequency), amount and age were different for Aboriginal participants, who often placed an event in time by referring to other things occurring at the time, not to the year or their age. Simulated interactions with an interpreter also revealed that, at times, it appears there are no equivalent words in the Aboriginal language to explain ideas adequately. These factors support what other authors have stated, for example Eades (1982) and Harkins (1995) regarding questions and answers, Devitt and McMasters (1998a) and Fenwick and Stevens (2004) regarding Aboriginal people's use of silence, and Trudgen (2000) regarding misunderstanding medical terms. They also contribute a concrete example of interactions that have been analysed and reveal multiple factors in miscommunication between non-Aboriginal health professionals and Aboriginal participants from remote communities operating together.

Views of illness causation

Aboriginal people's responses to health professionals in the hospital setting are also partly dictated by cultural factors. While Aboriginal people do recognise causal relationships in ill health, such as poor diet, alcohol, and sugar in the case of renal disease, Devitt and McMasters (1998 p. 86) state:

> both patients and the wider Aboriginal community believe strongly that the ultimate causes of life-threatening illnesses are in the realms of nonnatural phenomena, including, but not limited to, pre-meditated acts of sorcery.

In a study carried out in the Alice Springs hospital, Fenwick and Stevens (2004) state that the Aboriginal people expected the nurses to conduct business similar to that of their own traditional tribal healers, *to see within* and to *just know* [author's emphasis] (2004 p. 24). Their responses, when questioned about pain, were to either turn their heads away or hide their head and/or body under a blanket. The authors suggest that nurse/patient interactions were misinterpreted due to cultural conflict. As a result, the nurses administered inadequate post-operative pain relief. It is also possible that the question-and-answer style of communication played a role in the miscommunication. The authors state that 'The nurses anticipated that the client would contribute to their own care by communicating pain experiences in ways that are familiar and are believed to be universal' (2004 p. 24).

Weeramanthri (1997) explores the perceptions of differences between Aboriginal and non-Aboriginal views on illness causation and death through interviews with non-Aboriginal medical practitioners working in remote communities in the Northern Territory. One doctor interviewed by Weeramanthri (1997 p. 1010) stated:

> I feel free and happy to discuss things from a Western perspective, but people do not believe in what I say … they have a quizzical look, maybe they don't understand the terminology, but most important, they just don't believe it … we're talking at cross purposes ...

There are many aspects of the Aboriginal view of illness and its causation which contribute to how Aboriginal people perceive their illness, and what they understand of non-Aboriginal explanations of illness causation. It is important for health professionals to understand that Aboriginal people may also hold dual views, derived from traditional understandings and western interpretations of illness causation.

Features of language and non-verbal cues that contribute to misunderstandings

Aboriginal patients have sometimes been labelled by non-Aboriginal health professionals as uncooperative, while Aboriginal people sometimes see non-Aboriginal health professionals as rude. These perceptions may be based on differences in *contextualisation cues*. Gumperz (1982) includes *contextualisation cues* as features of language such as intonation, speech rhythm, and a choice of *lexical, phonetic* and/or *syntactical* options that are needed to correctly interpret information one is being given. He (Gumperz 1982, p. 132) states that:

> When a difference in interpretation is brought to a participant's attention, it tends to be seen in attitudinal terms. A speaker is said to be unfriendly, impertinent, rude, uncooperative, or to fail to understand. Interactants do not ordinarily notice that the listener may have failed to perceive a shift in rhythm or a change in pronunciation.

Hall (1959, 1966) refers to the micro-analysis of non-verbal signs, attributing a large proportion of misunderstandings to supposedly minor facial signs and gestures. Scheflen (1972) has made a detailed study of body postures of patients and analysts in psychiatric interviews, including these as *contextualisation cues*. Different cultural groups place greater or lesser importance on non-verbal cues. A study of *contextualisation cues* in communication between Aboriginal patients and non-Aboriginal health professionals may reveal differences in perception based on different cues.

Ways forward

In order to improve health outcomes for Aboriginal patients, authors of the Sharing True Stories website (http://www.sharingtruestories.

com) suggest that it is essential for health care professionals to learn about their own communication practices, and to find out what is culturally specific in one's own communication process and content. Furthermore, it is necessary to question the extent of shared knowledge in the communication between practitioners and Aboriginal patients within the health context.

Action Research methodology may be useful to professionals and to patients in this study, because of its collaborative process between the researcher and the people in the situation using critical enquiry (Flood 1999). The cycles of planning, action, reflection and evaluation used in action research mean that communication and interviews of practitioners can be triangulated with the communication and interviews of patients and others relevant in a study of communication, with thematic analysis also being a useful tool of analysis. This methodology can be empowering, both for health professionals researchers. They are free to express their concerns which could ultimately lead to positive change.

Overview

This paper has focused on three areas of potential communication difficulty between non-Aboriginal health professionals and Aboriginal patients: use of western style question-and-answer sequences to communicate with Aboriginal patients; different views on health and illness and differences in communication cues. Some positive communication strategies have also been outlined. However, research is needed to analyse the difficulties that arise in communication, and to assess the impacts of miscommunication on service delivery to Aboriginal patients.

References

The Generational Health Review 2003, *Better Choices, Better Health: Final Report of the Generational Health Review—Summary*, South Australian Department of Human Services, Adelaide.

Cass, A, Lowell, A, Christie, M, Snelling, PL, Flack, M, Marrnganyin, B & Brown, I 2002, 'Sharing the true stories: improving communication between Aboriginal patients and healthcare workers' in *Medical Journal of Australia*, vol. 176, pp. 466–470.

Dawson, R 1987, *The Present State of Australia*, Archival Facsimiles Limited, Alburgh.

Devitt, J & McMasters, A (eds) 1998a, *Living on Medicine: a Cultural Study of End-stage Renal Disease among Aboriginal People*, I.A.D. Press, Alice Springs.

Devitt, J & McMasters, A (eds) 1998b, *On the Machine: Aboriginal Stories about Kidney Troubles*, I.A.D. Press, Alice Springs.

Eades, D 1982, 'You Gotta Know How to Talk ... information seeking in South-East Queensland Aboriginal society' in *Australian Journal of Linguistics*, vol. 2, pp. 61–82.

Edis, F 1998, *'Just Scratching the Surface: Miscommunication in Aboriginal Health Care'* Masters Report, Faculty of Education, Northern Territory University, viewed 17 August 2004, <http://www.sharingtruestories.com>

Fenwick, C & Stevens, J 2004, 'Post Operative Pain Experiences of Central Australian Women: What Do We Understand?' in *Australian Journal of Rural Health*, vol. 12, pp. 22–27.

Flood, RL 1999, *Rethinking the Fifth Discipline: Learning within the Unknowable*, Routledge, London.

Gumperz, J 1982, *Discourse Strategies*, Cambridge University Press, Cambridge.

Hall, ET 1959, *The Silent Language*, Doubleday, New York.

Hall, ET 1966, *The Hidden Dimension*, Doubleday, New York.

Harkins, J 1994, *Bridging Two Worlds: Aboriginal English and Cross-cultural Understanding*, University of Queensland Press, St Lucia.

Hassell, E 1975, *My Dusky Friends: Aboriginal life, customs and legends and glimpses of station life at Jarramungup in the 1880s*, CW Hassell, East Fremantle.

Heritage, J 2001, 'Goffman, Garfinkel and Conversation Analysis' in *Discourse Theory and Practice*, eds. M Wetherall, S Taylor & SJ Yates, Sage Publications, Newbury Park, pp. 47–56.

Malcolm IG & Koscielecki, MM, 1997, *Aboriginality and English: Report to the Australian Research Council*, Centre for Applied Language Research, Edith Cowan University, Mount Lawley.

Maynard, DW 1992, '"On Clinicians co-implicating recipients" perspective in the delivery of diagnostic news' in *Talk at Work: Interaction in Institutional settings*, eds P Drew & J Heritage, Cambridge University Press, Cambridge, pp. 331–358.

Millett, E 1980, *An Australian Parsonage or the Settler and the Savage in Western Australia*, University of Western Australia Press, Nedlands.

Ong, LML, DeHaes, JCJM, Hoos, AM & Lammes, FB 1995, 'Doctor-Patient Communication: A Review of the Literature' in *Social Science and Medicine*, vol. 40, no. 7, pp. 903–918.

Scheflen, AE 1972, *Body Language and the Social Order*, Prentice Hall, Englewood Cliffs.

Troy, J 1990, 'Australian Aboriginal Contact with the English language in New South Wales: 1788-1845', monograph in *Pacific Linguistics*, Series B, pp. 103.

Trudgen, R 2000, *Why Warriors Lie Down and Die,* Aboriginal Resource and Development Services, Darwin.

von Hugel, BC 1994, *New Holland Journal: November 1833 – October 1834* (Dymphna Clark Trans.), Melbourne University Press, Melbourne.

Watson, M 1987, 'The communication problems of tribal Aboriginal women in the maternity ward' in *Darwin Education Studies Department,* Darwin Institute of Technology, Darwin.

Weeramanthri, T 199,7 '"Painting a Leonardo with Finger Paint" Medical Practitioners Communicating about Death with Aboriginal People' in *Social Science and Medicine,* vol. 45, no. 7, pp. 1005-1015.

Why won't they talk? An investigation into learner reticence in English as a Second Language classrooms

Johanna Motteram

The causes of learner *reticence* in ESL classrooms are identified in this chapter. An analysis of classroom observations and transcripts of classroom talk were used to find these causes.

Reticence has not been clearly defined in the literature. There is a psychological sense of *reticence* and it seems the word has been borrowed from psychology, but a precise meaning relating to the ESL context has not been attributed to the word. Chen (2000) attempts a definition by contrasting *reticence* with active participation. However, this is not an adequate definition, because learners may be actively participating and silent. The *Concise Oxford Dictionary* (1989, p. 889) defines *reticence* as 'reserve in speech, avoidance of saying all one knows or feels, or more than is necessary'. In this chapter reticent students are considered reserved in speech, often silent and not actively participating and engaged.

The research took place over two weeks, in an intermediate level, general English class. The class members were from a variety of language backgrounds: Chinese, Japanese, Korean and Spanish. Their ages ranged from 18 to late 20s. The class was working through an intermediate level textbook, *New Headway* (2003) and the teacher selected additional materials to support the vocabulary and grammar focus of the text. In the classes observed the teacher chose materials that were intended to encourage small group interaction because she was aware that the focus of the research was on the learners' interactions.

Literature review

Studies of ESL/EFL classrooms have investigated student *reticence* and supplied a variety of explanations. Affective, cultural, linguistic, educational and situational causes have been identified as reasons for

Asian learners' *reticence* in English-speaking settings (Chen 2003, Cheng 2000, Liu & Littlewood 1997, Tsui 1996, Scovel 1994). In the Australian ESL context learners are often Asian. Therefore these descriptions of learners' *reticence* are relevant, even though much of the research described in these papers took place in an EFL setting.

Dinsmore (1985) looked closely at teacher talk and teacher-student interaction in several EFL classes in Japan. The classes were nominally communicative but largely teacher-centred and did not provide opportunities for students' personal meaning-making. His description of the classroom implied that there were very few opportunities for any real student-student interaction. Dinsmore also made reference to the IRE pattern of teacher-student interaction and drew conclusions about the restrictions this pattern makes on the possibility of real communication occurring in the classroom. Through classroom observations, recordings and subsequent discourse analysis of transcriptions of classroom talk, Dinsmore concluded that the lack of personal meaning-making opportunities and structured power relationships in Japanese EFL classrooms contributed to learners' *reticence*.

Further comment on IRE can be found in Hall and Walsh's (2002) article. They discuss the limitations of the IRE pattern and cite research which argues that adopting an IRF pattern of teacher-student interaction will provide more opportunities for student learning. Their basis for this distinction is that an IRF pattern may lead into an opening for instructional conversation. Conversely, an IRE pattern is likely to stop discourse, because there is no next step in the discourse pattern after the teacher's evaluation of the learner's response. If the teacher gives feedback to the learner's response, there is an opportunity for the learner to question the feedback. It is unlikely that the learner will question an evaluation unless they are looking for further linguistic information. Therefore, the content information exchange will stop.

Jackson (2001) investigated learner *reticence* in content-based case discussions in a Hong Kong university. Her research encompassed interviews of students and teachers, case discussion observations, survey results and analysis of classroom talk. Jackson's recommendations to teachers faced with student *reticence* focused on teacher behaviours (such as questioning style and time allowed for responses) and class management strategies (especially the use of small groups). She did not closely address small group interactions and what effect they may have on learner *reticence*. Jackson drew conclusions linking educational experience, cultural expectations of classroom behaviour and affective issues (such as confidence) with student *reticence* in English language case discussions.

Jones (1999) identified differences between academic and general discourse behaviour. He discusses specific aspects of academic discourse behaviour and the difficulties non-native speakers may find with academic discourse when they are working with native speaker discussion leaders. His data is based on surveys of Australian university lecturers, tutors and non-native speaker students and also on reading around cross-cultural issues, but he does not investigate closely what actually happens in tutorial discussions. Jones makes recommendations to discussion leaders and non-native speaker participants in academic group discussion in an attempt to resolve reticent behaviour. His recommendations include: modifying academic discourse behaviour to accept silence in the group; giving reticent learners an opportunity to formulate responses; and changing questioning styles.

Harklau (1999) discusses learner resistance to tasks within college ESL writing classes. While Harklau does not speak specifically of *reticence* in her description of resistance, she mentions resistance in settings where learners do not value tasks or have not had the value of tasks explicitly signposted. She also mentions resistance in contexts where the learners' background has not been considered by the teacher when the task has been formulated. This idea could be transposed to consider classroom *reticence* as a form of resistance. Jones (1999) also mentions the need for teachers to consider learners' background and experience when teaching.

Storch's (2002) research investigated *dyadic* interaction within an Australian university-based ESL classroom. Her data was a collection of audio recordings of the *dyadic* interaction in a variety of tasks over a period of thirteen weeks. Her analysis is based on a sociocultural view of learning and describes relationships of learners within groups and how their interaction influenced their learning. She describes *dyadic* interaction by the roles that learners take as they complete a task. Within her descriptions she mentions the opportunity for a 'dominant/passive pattern of interaction' (Storch 2002, p.133). In her analysis of transcriptions of a dominant/passive pair the talking time is very unbalanced, with the dominant member ignoring the passive members' suggestions and interrupting. When considering small group work it can be seen that interaction between dominant and passive members of a group will result in learner *reticence*. Storch (2002 p.135) also identifies an 'expert/novice' relationship within *dyadic* interaction. This relationship will also cause some learner *reticence* because the novice defers to the experts' opinion and allows them speaking rights. While Storch s research is restricted by its measurement of learning being reduced to grammatical components of language and her data being drawn primarily from transcripts of pair work unsupported by field observations, she does supply some possible explanations for learner *reticence*.

A *sociocultural* perspective is taken by others such as Donato (2000), Swain, Brooks and Tocalli-Beller (2002), and De Guerrero and Villamil (2000). *Sociocultural* theory describes language learning as taking place through participation in a zone of proximal development with a more knowledgeable leader. The leader's behaviours which enhance learning are described as *scaffolding*. These papers discuss the possibility of peer-to-peer *scaffolding*, whereby learners work in pairs or groups and one of the learners takes the role of expert. Evidence of peer-to-peer *scaffolding* was observed in some learners' gestures.

A different perspective on *reticence* can be found in Miller's (1999) research into how language is used to construct *identity*, which shows migrant high school students on a continuum from silence to audibility as they gradually make their voices heard in English. Miller discusses how the learners were able to construct an appropriate *discourse identity* as they moved from intensive English classes to mainstream schools. Miller's subjects explained how, as they became more proficient in spoken English, they were able to make friends with native speakers and find a place in their new schools. Miller identifies English proficiency as the key to the learners' integration in their new schools, because it is linked to their ability to speak for themselves and express their individuality. ESL students with limited English proficiency may find it difficult to construct an *identity* in English discourse and may therefore be restricted to behaving reticently.

The review of literature began in investigating CLT and its applicability in non-Western cultures. Through CLT's emphasis on spoken interaction came the expectation that learners would participate in speaking activities in the classroom. When learners do not participate in these activities their behaviour is assessed because the teacher's expectation is that they will participate. Coupled with the CLT teacher's expectation is the understanding of *sociocultural* theory according to which language is learned through learners' active participation with more knowledgeable partners. Further reading into collaboration in the classroom led to the question of why, at times, learners did not participate in small group work. Considering that speaking is very often the focus of small group work, this led to the question of why learners do not speak. This question is the basis for this research.

Research aims

The original intention was to investigate linguistic reasons for student *reticence* in the classroom. However, following observations identified that it was not possible to distinguish linguistic reasons from other reasons in such a small-scale study.

It was also identified that investigating linguistic reasons for *reticence* was a reductionist approach. Harris' (1998) theory of *Integrational* Linguistics inspires consideration of all aspects of an idea. It was reductionist to expect to be able to explain student *reticence* in terms of interaction management skills alone because all discourse needs to be considered in its social and cultural contexts. Fairclough (1989) also pointed out the narrowness of the research because 'social conditions determine properties of discourse' (p. 19).

From this a more open question was derived: what causes for learner *reticence* can be deduced from a small-scale study of an ESL class? Or, in other words why won't they talk?

Methodology

Social interaction with the teacher provided an opportunity to request permission to observe her class. The research *aims* had not been refined at that stage, but it was clear classroom-based research would be needed. The teacher was interested in this because she had recently completed the *Certificate of English Language Teaching to Adults* and had just started her first paid ESL teaching position.

A copy of an earlier paper on research into student *reticence* was provided to the teacher to introduce her to similar thoughts on language learning and classroom research. A subsequent meeting decided that in return for observing her lessons she would like feedback on her teaching, copies of the transcripts and a copy of the paper before it was submitted.

The Director of Studies at the school was also provided with the research *aims*, the proposed methodology and background. Permission to observe in the school was granted after writing to the Principal. Before the observations began, permission from the students to record and write about their classes was also granted.

A timetable of observation sessions was negotiated with the teacher and three sessions took place over a two-week period. Before each of the lessons observed the teacher explained the material she had chosen and provided a brief lesson plan. After each lesson the teacher was given some feedback on the lesson, including some comments on classroom management, material selection and adapting plans during lessons to reflect student engagement with topics or activities.

Lessons were observed from the teacher's left as she stood at the board. The students were seated in a 'U' shape and from this position most of the students' faces and the teacher's actions could be observed. Two tape recorders were used to record most of the three observations. Field notes recorded seating patterns, body positioning, timing of the lessons, turn-taking behaviours (self or other selection) and miscellaneous items of attention.

Small group work was closely observed in groups which formed near the observation position. Movement from the observer was restricted, other than to reposition the tape recorders, because drawing further attention to the observation could potentially change behaviour from the students.

After each observation parts of the recordings were transcribed, the selection of which was based on the field notes. Recordings of groups that were not observed were not transcribed. After the first attempt at transcription, it was identified that the subsequent observations of the small group interaction needed to identify the speakers and carry a brief description of their turns as the discussion progressed (Swann 1994). The second and third transcriptions benefited from that change in observation practice.

Data Analysis and Discussion

Close reading of the transcriptions of the lessons coupled with the field notes led to the following analysis of *reticence* in this ESL classroom.

Reticence and choice of task

Implementation of a textbook task which resulted in reticent behaviour from many class members was observed in Observation One. The task was introduced by the teacher describing and displaying her favourite piece of jewellery. During the introduction the students were engaged and actively listening. Students watched closely as she took the ring around and showed it to them; some asked questions about the ring. Following the description of the ring, the teacher directed the students to their textbooks. At this stage many of the learners were visibly disengaged. One placed his head on his desk, another looked very sleepy. Some sighed or yawned loudly and most of the students had vacant or unhappy expressions. When the teacher asked for input there was no response to her request.

Analysis of the textbook task led to the conclusion that it was a formulaic and superficial task with a meaningless prediction exercise to prepare learners for a listening phase (McCarthy and Carter 1994).

Within this criticism of the textbook task are the following issues:

- The text book was culturally biased towards a Eurocentric world view; themes included European classical musical history and instruments (Beethoven and baby grand pianos) and European geography; which led to later discussion of content as an influence on learner *reticence*.
- The text introduced four white, 30-40 year old, middle-class speakers with whom it was difficult for the mostly Asian, 18-25 year old learners to identify.
- The spoken text was scripted and not an example of a real spoken genre and therefore not easily identified as an important text to understand and produce.

Following the students' retreat from the task, the teacher reacted by starting to echo learners' contributions. This may have compounded the *reticence* issue because the episode did not represent real communication. Later the teacher asked the students to 'make a sentence' when they responded (data from field notes) which led to further silence. These two teacher reactions emphasised the difference between various phases of the lesson. The whole class' *reticence* in response to this task can be interpreted as a rejection of the listening exercises in the textbook as a classroom exercise.

Reticence and power

As the atmosphere of the classroom changed when the given task was textbook-based, it could also be argued that the power relationships changed in that transition.

Earlier in the lesson the students participated in small group discussions. In most of the groups this meant they could contribute their own ideas freely and experience a flat power structure.

In the textbook phase a more traditional task and power structure was introduced. The teacher reassumed the role of instruction giver and task setter. The students then needed to listen to the instructions and comply with her requests. As the focus of the lesson became the textbook, the possibility of multiple correct answers which occurred during the co-construction of the recount ended and a phase began where only one correct answer was possible. One consequence of these traditional power structures and classroom roles is that learners adopt the passive roles that they are accustomed to taking as a result of their educational background (Jackson 2001, Chowdhury 2003).

In this situation it seemed that the students sat back in their chairs and expected the teacher to take the active role. This has been described as an expectation of 'the teacher as the sage on the stage' (Chen 2003, p. 270).

The teacher's reaction to the learners adopting these passive roles, in this episode, was to become more authoritarian in an attempt to force longer turns on the learners' part. This spiralling of reticent behaviour (perhaps as resistance to the textbook task or as resistance to the change in their status in the classroom) made the atmosphere uncomfortable for all involved.

The textbook activity is based on students listening to a tape recording and extracting information about its content. This activity is based on a *dichotomist* view, where there is a correct and incorrect answer to a problem. In this activity the students know that the teacher holds the power because they are the one who will decide which answers are correct. This disenfranchisement of the students resulted in a reticent recoil.

Reticence and choice of topic

A non-threatening task of ranking companies in terms of least preferred investments became one of the most surprising interactions in the observations. When asked to state which companies the group considered least likely to show good medium term investment returns, group member L nominated Playboy Enterprises. The topic was taken up by S as an opportunity to exert power over M through her questioning of his consumption of pornography.

In the following transcription it is evident that the three speakers are engaging in an exclusive discussion accessible only to speakers with experience of and expertise in flirtation. The discourse also excludes speakers without a close personal relationship with the other speakers because of the personal nature of the topic. This meant that two of the six members of the group were excluded because they had recently joined the class and did not have the requisite personal relationships for participation.

Observation Three transcription (M is a Japanese male, C and S are Korean females)

1. **L** worst, *Playboy ((laugh))*
2. **M** *Playboy*
3. **C & S** ((laugh))
4. **M** I like *Playboy* but I think that
5. **S** how many Play, *Playboy* books do you have?
6. **M** how many?
7. **S** in homestay
8. **M** in homestay?
9. **S** homestay [
10. **C** or in Japan]
11. **M** no
12. **C** no?
13. **M** no, not many, I don't know
14. **S** how many times do you watch Playboy station

15. C ((laugh))
16. S program in Japan
17. M I can't, I can't watch Playboy program
18. S why?
19. M do you have, do you have Playboy program in Korea?
20. S if I pay
21. C you pay?
22. M no, no, no, no. because we also have to pay but I don't want to pay, pay about Playboy program
23. C ( )so Internet, Internet
24. S probably you have five or ten *Playboy* magazines in your house?
25. C ((laughs))
26. M do you know?
27. S one no
28. M I think, I think, I have, I have good magazine, better than *Playboy*
29. C & S ((laugh))
30. M not necessary just *Playboy*
31. S you are teenager, probably you, probably you teenage
32. M I'm not sure, yeah, probably

In this extract group member S takes a powerful role in the discussion. She takes power by questioning a male about his consumption of pornography, a strong taboo for women. She also repeats her question and overrides C's introduction of Internet access to pornography (line 23) when it seems that M may avoid answering (line 24). S continues her questioning in line 31 until M concedes that he did own *Playboy* magazines as a teenager.

Another interesting facet of this sample is that the speaker who introduced the topic in line 1 subsequently lost control of the topic. It was interesting to see how long L would be willing to be silent, because she was generally a very dominant group member. In the next line in the transcript L introduces a new topic to the other silent members of the group and controls a side discussion.

The *reticence* of Y and H can be attributed in part to their lack of close personal relationships with the other members, because they are *New-Arrivals* in the classroom. This observation took place on their second day in the classroom. Their *reticence* could also be explained by their ages (they are both younger than S and C). Related to this is the possibility that they may have had little experience of this style of cross-gender banter. During the episode both Y and H looked down at their papers. Duff (2002), Harklau (1999) and Chen (2003) considered the possibility of *reticence* being closely related with controversial topic choice.

The marginalisation of non-participants through social clique membership (as evidenced by S, M and C's interaction) can be interpreted as both an example of *reticence* due to topic and *reticence* due to lack of power in a small group. Further discussion with the teacher revealed that S has continued to use attention towards males as a tool to gain power in the classroom.

It is evident that choice of a taboo topic led to marginalisation and silence from half of a small group of six learners in Observation Three. While the topic selection was made by one of the later marginalised learners, the treatment of the topic by S, C and M resulted in a split of the group.

Reticence in small group discussion

An episode where two pairs, A (Male) and S (Male), N (Female) and M (Female), merged to work on a narrative, displayed a group with unequal power relationships. The task required the four students to explain how changes between two pictures of the same room had occurred over time. When the groups merged (the girls moved their seats to join the two boys in their position in the classroom), A took the role of group leader and explained to the new members that their input was not required because he had already formulated the answer to the task. He then told the girls his interpretation of events.

Observation One transcription (A is a Japanese male, S is a Korean male, Girls are Chinese)

1.	**A**	ok, ok girls I'm sorry but the mystery has been already resolved
2.	**S**	resolved
3.	**Girls**	((laugh))

4.	**A**	I think, ah, at this moment the window has been, already broken, someone, someone broke into the house, if someone wanted to break into the more narrow hole, the window it's too small, small
5.	**Girls**	ok, mmhmm
6.	**A**	maybe they can't through
7.	**Girls**	ok
8.	**A**	I think this, that is for women
9.	**Girls**	mm
10.	**A**	maybe maybe, ehh, she is woman
11.	**Girls**	((laugh))
12.	**Girl**	( ) is woman
13.	**A**	( )
14.	**Girl**	somebody, somebody come
15.	**A**	by paper plane ((laughter)), took the paper, to the girl, 10. and this is letter and he was writing a letter to her to break up with her and, and at the same time she came and she get angry and killed him by umm the ( ) knife and ( )
16.	**Girls**	((laugh))
17.	**A**	... and to this, to this took the car radio, I think there is no reason, no reason to steal the car radio
18.	**Girl**	( )
19.	**S**	but car radio is very heavy, very heavy no
20.	**Girl**	maybe, maybe
21.	**A**	and after she killed him she ( ) back to and drew but she scatterbrain so she lost her hand bag because she came here to
22.	**Girl**	mmmm get this bag

Close reading of the transcript shows that not only does A control the discourse by telling the girls their input is not needed, but also through his telling of the story he gives the female members of his group some idea of how he thinks about women. In line 8 he tells them that a woman would be small enough to get through a small hole in a window, in line 16 a woman who has been broken up with will be angry to the point of violently murdering her boyfriend, and in line 23 he tells them a woman is scatterbrained.

This is an example of a dominant member of the group controlling the discourse and not allowing others to speak (line 1). The other members of the group allow the dominant learner to hold the floor but their reasons for this would be varied. It is possible to make assumptions based on the other learners' gender, nationality and speaking prowess, however, without interviewing the silent learners it is not possible to draw any conclusions. It is just as possible that the silent learners didn't have any strong opinions on the exercise and felt it was easier to allow A to speak and report for them. Or that after listening to his construction of the exercise they felt it was safer to stay quiet.

During the observations, L was a dominant member of groups. She often controlled discourse by speaking first and then nominating other members to supply their information. She also spoke for other members of her group at times by answering questions directed at them.

In the following episode, L is dominating the interaction by taking long turns and then by nominating another of her group members to answer a difficult question. She also ignores an interruption by the teacher to continue her turn along the course she has set.

Observation Two transcription (L is a Chinese female; S, C and H are Korean females; M is a Japanese male)

1.	**L**	What company do you choose?
2.	**S**	McDonalds and Mercedes Benz, you choose Global Life?
3.	**L**	No, we choose ( ) oil because oil is very important for our and ( ) and he choose Sony
4.	**C**	Sony
5.	**M**	yeah
6.	**C**	why?
7.	**S**	decrease?
8.	**M**	no, no, no, no
9.	**C**	((laughs))
10.	**L**	no, ok, we choose chemical company and electronics and Bank of America and Fifth National Bank and Transworld Airlines and IBM and ITT International Telephone and Telegraph, and Columbia Broadcasting System and ( ) and Krupp Armaments.

11. **Teacher**	do you know what this means, weapons, it means weapons
12. **L**	and ( ) and Kaiser Aluminium, we choose ( ) and more and more important things we choose
13. **M**	mmm
14. **Teacher**	and have you told them why you chose things
15. **C**	why did you choose the companies
16. **L**	mmm
17. **C**	why did you choose?

At line 10 and line 12 L returns the group to the task by continuing to list the companies in which her group chose to invest. by keeping the discussion on topic and following the handout's directions, L was able to control the group discussion.

These cases of a dominant group member controlling the discussion and taking long turns in the reporting back phases of the tasks has an impact on the other students. When L takes long, grammatically unsophisticated turns she deprives other members of her group of speaking time and the already resolved content of the report. This means that if they wish to speak they must address ideas that are more difficult to express and they may not have much time left to do so. She also controls the discourse by nominating who is going to speak next, which leaves the other members without simple access to contribution.

Reticence related to lack of understanding

There were many instances during the observations when learners were reticent because they did not understand the directions. Often the learners were able to find out from their classmates what was happening. Only M would ask the teacher if he did not understand the task. Often this lack of comprehension was linked with learner tardiness and this was resolved when the teacher enforced the school policy regarding late arrivals.

Teacher's perception of reticence

Before entering the classroom for the second observation the teacher explained that there were two new students in the class, Y (Japanese female) and H (Korean female). She described them as female, Asian and quiet, noting that Y was especially quiet.

Jones (1999), as well as Dwyer and Heller-Murphy (1996), discusses the expectation some teachers have that particular students will be reticent. It is possible that when teachers enter the classroom with these prejudices they can be a self-fulfilling prophecy.

Before the lesson began, Y and H were asked for their permission to be observed and recorded in the classroom. Often in the second observation, Y concentrated very hard on closely watching the other members of the group to try and follow their interactions. Because this was Y's second day in the class and she had no prior experience of this style of learning, she needed to work hard to try understand the expectations of the classroom. While Y was actively engaged in trying to understand the discourse conventions of the small group, whenever the teacher approached the group she looked down at her book. It is possible that she did this in an effort not to be nominated and hence evaluated by the teacher (Jackson 2001). After the lesson, this behaviour was discussed with the teacher who said that Y had been looking down and not participating all the time.

A different explanation of Y's *reticence* can be posited when the following episode is considered with a *sociocultural* perspective. In this episode a small group of four members collaboratively participated in the socialisation of two new members of the class. During the episode the socialisation was mainly achieved through non-verbal turn nomination of the two new members by the two more experienced members.

The field notes recorded the turn taking behaviour as follows:

- S starts then asks J
- J speaks, lots of hands to express
- Y checks dictionary
- J nudges Y to start her turn
- S points to H to start her turn
- S self-selects
- J self-selects
- S interrupts to support J.

During the discussion Y and H alternated between watching S and J closely and looking at their papers to try and follow the interaction.

If Y or H were not watching S and J, they were nudged to prompt them to start their turns. While observing this interaction it was evident that the experienced members were working together to show the new members the right time for them to speak.

This is evidence of cooperative *scaffolding* to help the new members participate in small group discussion. Galbraith, Van Tassel and Wells (1999) describe similar situations of cooperative *scaffolding* in a classroom when more competent class members explained language functions to other less competent members.

There are many other mentions of peer-to-peer *scaffolding* in the relevant literature (De Guerro & Villamil 2000, Swain & Lapkin 1998). This example differs from those examples in as much as the scaffolders used physical prompts not words to enable their less competent peers to contribute to the discussion. Perhaps this is another example of the benefit of having an observer in the classroom, who has no other role to play, because data which comes only from tape recordings will miss this type of behaviour.

If a *sociocultural* perspective is taken on language learning, then this instance of *scaffolding* may explain in part of how language learning takes place. If so, then *reticence* throughout the class discourse can be described in these terms. Lack of *scaffolding* by the teacher and choice of language beyond learners' zones of proximal development may be two primary reasons for learners' *reticence*.

Reticence and teacher talk

The following extract highlights a few of the issues related to teacher talk, which are relevant to learner *reticence* in this classroom.

In line 3 the teacher asks the learners a very difficult question about a list of vocabulary. The student response is silence, perhaps because they do not want to answer in case they are wrong, or because they have no idea of a possible answer. In Observation Three there was another marked example of questioning beyond students' reasonably expected knowledge, when the teacher attempted to elicit vocabulary related to banking and finance. This attempt was also met with silence.

In lines 1, 2 and 3; 5, 6 and 8; 9 and 10; and 11 and 12 there are examples of IRE patterns of interaction. This style of interaction is prevalent in classrooms (Hall & Walsh 2002).

When an IRE pattern of interaction is followed, the teacher holds the power, the answers and the right to accept or reject student contributions. When students are then asked to contribute, they may become reticent because they know that they are at risk of being negatively evaluated or rejected.

Observation One transcription

1.	**Teacher**	stop being naughty or I'll get the wooden spoon, ok, no I won't, ok, so what can you tell me about that column of words, those words, where is the stress?
2.	**S**	second word
3.	**Teacher**	ok, why, why do you think, -(4)- what do the first words, what do these words tell us -(5)- What does the first word tell us about the second word, -(4)- it tells us what it's made of, sauce, made of tomatoes, sandwich, made of cheese, hat made of straw, spoon made of wood
4.	**Students**	oh
5.	**Teacher**	the other thing, there is another word we didn't pick up out of this picture is front door, front door, a, another time when we put the stress on the second word, not the first word is when it's telling you where, where the thing is located for example front door we don't say front door we say front door, front door car radio is the same ( ) ok so, can you think of another example of a word that might go over here -(5)- a compound noun, a noun that is made up of two nouns that tells us where it is or what it's made of, front door
6.	**D**	fried rice
7.	**Students**	((Laugh))
8.	**Teacher**	no, that one doesn't fit D does it, fried rice, fried rice, fried rice, ok, wow that's telling us how the rice is cooked but not what it's made of, mmm -(5)-
9.	**S**	arm chair
10.	**Teacher**	arm chair, no, I don't think that fits either, front door, back door
11.	**S**	plastic bag

12. **Teacher** very good, plastic bag, plastic bag
13. **S** ( )
14. **Teacher** plastic bag, plastic bag everybody, plastic bag
15. **Students** plastic bag
16. **Teacher** beautiful, now, did you notice that some of these compound nouns are separate words, some are together and some, what's this thing called, here -(4)-
17. **S** hyphen

These types of examples of teacher talk contributing to learner *reticence* have been investigated before by other researchers (for example, Dinsmore 1985), however, they provide a limited explanation of *reticence* in the whole class. Teacher talk is one issue which needs to be considered amongst the range of other interactions in the classroom.

Reticence and physical issues

At times learners were seated in a row and asked to work together in groups of three or more. As the learners did not move to face each other this made group work difficult because they could not make eye contact and read each other's body language.

Often new groups were formed by merging existing dyads. At times this meant that only half of the group had to relocate and this may have led to feelings of core membership or self- nomination of dominant students as leaders when they did not have to move.

Learners in this classroom relied on electronic dictionaries. At times they were too busy looking up vocabulary to participate in the discussions around them.

Overview

Research into student *reticence* is limited because it has not employed classroom-based research to investigate precisely what is happening. Studies based on surveys of teachers and learners are restricted, because they rely on memory and perceptions.

This study has found that many explanations for learner *reticence* can be deduced from analysis of classroom observations and transcriptions of classroom talk. *Reticence* can result from unequal power relationships between teacher and student and student and student, topic choice that marginalises learners, teacher preconceptions, and early stages of learner socialisation.

Future research into *reticence* which takes these factors into account may produce useful recommendations to teachers of non-native speakers who are faced with learner *reticence*. This research should provide opportunities for learners to discuss their reticent behaviour with researchers to ensure that conclusions drawn by the researchers are supported by learners' experiences.

References

Chen, T 2003, 'Reticence in class and on-line: two ESL students' experiences with communicative language teaching' in *System*, vol. 31, no. 2, pp. 259–281.

Cheng, X 2000, 'Asian students' reticence revisited' in *System*, vol. 28, no. 3, pp. 435–446.

Chowdhury, R 2003, 'International TESOL training and EFL contexts: The cultural disillusionment factor' in *Australian Journal of Education*, vol. 47, no. 3, pp. 283–302.

De Guerrero, M & Villamil, O 2000, 'Activating the ZPD: Mutual Scaffolding in L2 Peer Revision' in *The Modern Language Journal*, vol. 84, no. 1 pp. 51–68.

Dinsmore, D 1985, 'Waiting for Godot in the EFL classroom' in *ELT Journal*, vol. 39, no. 4, pp. 225–234.

Donato, R 2000, 'Sociocultural contributions to understanding the foreign and second language classroom' in *Sociocultural Theory and Second Language Learning*, ed JP Lantolf, Oxford University Press, Oxford & New York, pp. 27–50.

Duff, PA 2002, 'The Discursive Co-Construction of Knowledge, Identity and Difference: An Ethnography of Communication in the High School Mainstream' in *Applied Linguistics*, vol. 23, no. 3 pp. 289–322.

Dwyer, E & Heller MA 1996, 'Japanese Learners in Speaking Classes' in *Edinburgh Working Papers in Applied Linguistics*, no. 7, pp. 46–55.

Fairclough, N 1989, *Language and Power*, Longman, London & New York.

Galbraith, B, Van Tassell, MA & Wells, G 1999 'On Learning With and From Our Students' in *Dialogic Inquiry: Toward a Sociocultural Practice and Theory of Education*, Cambridge University Press, Cambridge, pp. 293–312.

Hall, JK & Walsh, M 2002, 'Teacher-Student Interaction and Language Learning' in *Annual Review of Applied Linguistics*, vol. 22, pp. 186–203.

Harklau, L 1999, 'Representing Culture in the ESL Writing Classroom' in *Culture in Second Language Teaching and Learning*, ed E Hinkel, Cambridge University Press, Cambridge, pp. 109–130.

Harris, R 1998, Introduction *to Integrational Linguistics,* Pergamon, Oxford.
Jackson, J 2001, 'Reticence in second language case discussions: anxiety and aspirations' in *System,* vol. 30, no. 1, pp. 65–84.
Jones, JF 1999, 'From Silence to Talk: Cross Cultural Ideas on Students' Participation in Academic Group Discussion' in *English for Specific Purposes,* vol. 18, no. 3, pp. 243–259.
Liu, NF & Littlewood W 1997, 'Why do many students appear reluctant to participate in classroom learning discourse' in *System,* vol. 25, no. 3, pp. 371–384.
McCarthy, M & Carter, R 1994, 'Designing the discourse syllabus' in *Language as Discourse: Perspectives for Language Teaching,* Longman Group Limited, London.
Miller, J 1999, 'Becoming Audible: social identity and second language use' in *Journal of Intercultural Studies,* vol. 20 no. 2, pp. 149–165.
Scovel, T 1994, 'The Role of Culture in Second Language Pedagogy' in *System,* vol. 22, no. 2, pp. 205–219.
Soars, L & Soars, J 2003, *New Headway Intermediate,* Oxford University Press, Oxford.
Storch, N 2002, 'Patterns of Interaction in ESL Pair Work' in *Language Learning,* vol. 52, no. 1, pp. 119–158.
Swann, J 1994, 'Observation and Recording Talk in Educational Settings' in *Researching Language and Literacy in Social Context,* ed D Graddol, J Maybin, B Stierer, Multilingual Matters, Clevedon, pp. 26–48.
Swain, M, Brooks, L & Tocalli-Beller, A 2002, 'Peer-peer dialogue as a means of second language learning' in *Annual Review of Applied Linguistics,* vol. 22, pp. 171–185.
Swain, M & Lapkin, S 1998, 'Interaction and Second Language Learning: Two Adolescent French Immersion Students Working Together' in *The Modern Language Journal,* vol. 82, no. 3, pp. 320--337.
Sykes, JB (ed) 1989, *The Concise Oxford Dictionary,* Oxford University Press, Oxford.
Tsui, ABM 1991, 'Learner Involvement and Comprehensible Input' in *RELC Journal,* vol. 22, no. 2, pp. 44–60.
Yalden, J 1987, 'Discourse analysis and course design' in *Principles of Course Design for Language Teaching,* Cambridge University Press, Cambridge.

A pragmatic approach to editing and publishing at tertiary level

Ioana Petrescu and Judith Timoney

The current Australian editing market is facing a change of generations and concepts regarding the skills needed to be a good editor and how they can be acquired. Many editors learned the trade by doing, and developed their skills either in isolation or, sometimes, as apprentices in a publishing house. Some see a need for change, but others still think that the new academic degrees that have appeared in the last decade cannot actually teach what practice does.

There is also a transitional generation of editors, who, as Janet Mackenzie states in *The Editor's Companion* 'is a forty-ish, highly qualified, highly experienced woman with her own business … Many reported relevant experience, the most common being as a researcher, teacher or trainer, author or writer, librarian and journalist.' (p 14)

Responding to a growing demand for editing courses, many Australian universities have introduced in their curricula editing and publishing courses at different levels. At the University of South Australia, Editing and Publishing is a submajor and trains up to 30 editors each year. Most of them are female and take the course with a view to becoming freelancers working from home. Others find work in the Public Services, and in the last few years several graduates found work in big publishing houses or at top-shelf magazines.

The greatest challenge for them was to persuade employers that their knowledge and skills could compete with those of editors who had worked for many years in the field. Our students needed a publications record to go with their academic record in order to become competitive in the work market.

The method

The editing and publishing courses at UniSA respond to this need through a new approach and structure. In the first semester course,

Editing and Publishing, students acquire theoretical and practical knowledge in editing several types of writing. In the second semester course, Advanced Editing and Publishing, they apply their knowledge and skills working on real projects, sourced from the community and then published in the industry

As a teacher of creative and professional writing, editing and publishing within an undergraduate BA program, and as a supervisor of Honours and postgraduate students, my approach to teaching and learning is based on a belief that theory and practice must be linked and that students should have every opportunity to undertake activities which extend their skills in relation to the community and the professional world in which they work or will work. A vital element in the approach is to encourage and demonstrate collaborative engagement among students and with the industry partners with whom we work.

The students get acquainted with major resources in editing and publishing, such as the *Style manual for authors editors and printers* (6th edition, John Wiley and Sons Australia, Ltd, 2002); Janet Mackenzie, *The Editor's Companion* (CUP, 2004); Elizabeth Flann & Beryl Hill, *The Australian Editing Handbook* (Fully revised and updated 2nd edition, John Wiley and Sons Australia, Ltd, 2004); Lynne Spender, *Between the Lines: A Legal Guide for Writers and Illustrators* (Australian Society of Authors, Keesing Press, 2004), to name just a few. The students are also introduced to the SA Society of Editors, the SA Writers' Centre, and the Australian Association of Writing Programs, thus being encouraged to become a part of local and national networks in writing, editing and publishing.

This approach to teaching editing and publishing links synergistically the academic tradition with the current industry scene, thus empowering the students twice: the courses give the students both the advantage of sound theoretical knowledge, and the practical skills that are appreciated by employers. This is realised through the implementation of an innovative curriculum model that is cyclic and works from engagement with the industry. Real writing projects created in class are published commercially and then returned as key texts in the curriculum.

Publications that resulted from the Advanced Editing and Publishing course and followed this methodology are:

- *Heart of the Matter: An Introduction to Eighteen South Australian Poets* (Lythrum Press, Adelaide, 2005)—a book of interviews, reflective and exegetical pieces written by students of the Poetry course and edited by students in the Advanced Editing course;
- *Talk of the Town*, Lythrum Press, Adelaide, 2004—a collaborative project with David Homer, the book is a collection of pieces written for the Professional and Creative Communication course Writing the City, and edited in Advanced Editing;
- *The house that words built*, Lythrum Press, Adelaide, 2005—a collection of short stories written in the course Writing and Reading Texts B: Short Fiction and edited in Advanced Editing, the book is now a key text in my course Writing and Reading Texts B: Short Fiction;
- *Fuse or fracture: English as a world lingua franca* (linguistics reader published internally)—a collaborative project with Dr Mia Stephens, the book is a collection of linguistics articles written by students in linguistics courses and edited in Advanced Editing, and is now a key text in the course Language and Context;
- *Orrmulum*: newsmagazine published internally. The newsmagazine is now online and can be accessed at www.orrmulum.com.

The way I designed and applied the creative writing, editing and publishing courses in class led to the students' integration in the community, contact with the industry and production of specialism-specific outcomes even before graduation. The creative writing and editing students now have publications to their names and employers appreciate their CVs, which give our graduates an extra edge in the competitive professional work market. Editing and Publishing students are prepared now for work as professionals in the industry even before graduation. The editing and publishing courses facilitate active learning in industry contexts; foster both teamwork and independent learning; commit students to ethical action and social responsibility; and enhance effective communication skills.

The task

This book is the product of collaboration with my esteemed colleague,

Dr Peter Mickan, Head of Linguistics at the University of Adelaide. I was looking for a project for my editing and publishing class for the following year, and Dr Mickan was in need of an editor to put together a book comprising the valuable materials that had been accumulated from his teaching and supervision practice over several years. We agreed to produce the book together and Dr Mickan sent me several papers for editing. This became one of the projects in the Advanced Editing class and six students expressed their interest in being part of the book editing team. They read the papers, accepted what they believed was material of general interest and was adequately written too, edited the respective papers, and produced a book file ready for printing.

Judith Timoney, the team leader for this project, describes the process in more detail in the section below. She also refers to the challenges the editors encountered and overcame in their work with the selected materials. I will discuss here only one aspect of the process, which in my opinion was the most challenging and was resolved very professionally by the team.

Several chapters in this book are written by EFL writers. Some are papers that these Masters or PhD candidates presented at conferences and symposia, and thus presented a double challenge to the editors: addressing the ESL issues, while at the same time adhering to the Australian editors' code of ethics. According to the Australian Standards for Editing Practice there are five types of editing:

- A, The Publishing Process, Conventions and Industry Practice
- B, Management and Liaison
- C, Substance and Structure
- D, Language and Illustrations
- E, Completeness and Consistency. (Mackenzie, p 10)

Even though these were not theses but papers submitted for a book, because they were produced in an academic context the editors decided to adhere to the Council of the Australian Society of Editors' recommendations that 'the scope of editorial work should be restricted to matters covered in Standards D and E of Australian Standards for Editing Practice' (see Appendix in Mackenzie, pp 189–199). This meant that no editing of substance or structure could be done, and the editors addressed matters classified under categories

D and E, i.e. Language and Illustrations, and Completeness and Consistency.

Student-editors encountered several challenges in applying the criteria to texts written by ESL speakers. They had numerous meetings where they decided on whether light editing would suffice, what needed to be done to keep the voice of the author, and how best to proceed so as to produce a coherent book without altering the text through substantive or structural editing. The student-editors need to be commended for their professionalism, care and respect for the text and the authors.

The editing process from the perspective of the student team leader, Judith Timoney

As the student team leader of the linguistics book project, my first objective was to make sure that the principles studied in the Editing and Publishing course were put into practice while working on a real world project in the Advanced Editing course. The articles written by Dr Mickan's higher degree students were stimulating, and also challenging from the editor's point of view.

From the beginning, our editing team had two main objectives: to use a reader-centred approach and to make minimal changes to the author's work. The readers' needs dictated the editing decisions. We wanted to ensure that each article was simple to follow, and that the text was clear and easy to read.

Using the *Style manual*, our first task was to devise a house style to ensure consistency in layout, margins, fonts, titles, spacing and abbreviations. As the project progressed, the team constantly revised the house style to cover issues that had not been anticipated at the beginning. Some points seemed minor, yet were very important in giving the book a uniform appearance.

For example, well into the project several team members realised there was little consistency in the presentation of transcripts of dialogues. At issue was the use of colons. The team discussed whether or not there should be a colon after the name of each turn-taker. Since we had agreed upon a minimalist approach at the beginning, we opted to omit the colon and to put the turn-taker's name in bold. Attention to detail can be time consuming, but it is very important to the overall look of the book. Small points such as this frequently arose, which required further changes to the house style. In all, the house style was revised five times.

In keeping with our reader-centred approach, we decided that each article should be read by more than one person. While each team member worked in depth on the article(s) assigned to them, they were also involved in looking at other members' articles. We e-mailed each other our assigned articles and discussed them at length in regular meetings. There were many instances where team members offered valuable advice on pieces other than their own. For example, certain statements made by authors were ambiguous to some team members but not to others. While it took a lot of time, cross-editing proved to be a very useful exercise. Without doubt, the more people read a piece of work, the better the outcome was.

Success relies on good communication between team members. At the beginning of the project we each set up on our university e-mail accounts a distribution list, comprising all the team members. We would e-mail each other to arrange meetings as well as ask advice about editing issues. As the team leader, I always sent e-mails to the whole group, even if they were really only relevant to one or two team members. It was a way of keeping everyone 'in the loop' and apprised of everything occurring in the project. I stored all the e-mails I had sent and received in a folder on my computer, deleting them only at the conclusion of the course.

During group discussions, the most common problem encountered in the papers was wordiness, which frequently affected the clarity of the text. It was very challenging at times to make the language clearer without changing the text substantially. Problems with wordiness were solved in a number of ways: altering sentence structure; eliminating unnecessary words; and where possible, using the active rather than passive voice.

Altering sentence structure usually involved turning one large sentence into two or three smaller ones. Where there were sentences that contained several ideas, we broke them down, so each sentence contained only one idea. This greatly improved sentence clarity. In *The New Oxford Guide to Writing*, Thomas Kane offers many useful suggestions for eliminating wordiness in sentence construction. One I found particularly useful was, 'In general you should aim first at clarity, then strive for simplicity and concision' (p. 191). Frequently, though not always, achieving the first will result in the other two.

A simple but effective way of making the articles more reader-centred was to increase the number of headings and insert subheadings where necessary. It meant little or no change to the authors' words but improved both the readability and the appearance of the pieces, especially in instances where there were several pages of unbroken text. Reep (1997, p. 111) considers headings useful because they 'call attention to specific topics; provide an outline that helps readers see hierarchical relationships; help readers find specific data and show where changes in topics occur.'

There were several instances where excessive wordiness prevented our understanding of the material. Dr Mickan put us in contact with our authors and we were able to discuss areas where we had difficulties. I found this valuable for two reasons: firstly, I was able to clear up comprehension problems, and secondly, I was able to discuss the article at length with the author of the piece I was editing, which gave me a better idea of what she was trying to communicate to the reader. Coming from a non-English-speaking background, she had found it difficult to convey in English the highly theoretical basis of her paper. Throughout the course, Dr Petrescu stressed the importance of editors maintaining regular contact with their clients. For this project in particular, I found it was very important.

The editing team frequently discussed the authors' use of graphics, specifically tables, figures and diagrams. Two main problems were identified: the graphics were not relevant to the author's argument or there was not enough explanation provided to make them useful for the reader. After careful consideration and discussions with the authors, several team members altered some graphics and deleted others. Most graphics were very useable once they were clearly labelled and properly explained. Kress (1997, p. 62) advises writers to carefully consider the function of any visuals they include in their texts. Whether they provide information or illustration, their purpose must be made clear to the reader.

Once all the articles had been edited, I assembled them into one document and inserted a glossary, a contents page, and also a list of references that a team member, EL Benn, had prepared. I checked the document to see that everyone had conformed to the house style. This is a lengthy task and it is important to allow sufficient time to peruse the document properly. The easiest way for me was to go through the document many times, checking for one item/issue at a time, for example, headings, spacing or abbreviations. I found it unproductive to try to check everything in one reading.

I have enjoyed being involved in this project from its beginning through to its completion. It has furthered my interest in editing academic writing and provided me with real world experience in the area. It has been a pleasure working with Dr Mickan and Dr Petrescu, and I am grateful for their help and guidance.

Recommendations

An unexpected product of the editing process was a list of recommendations for EFL beginner writers of Academic English, that we, as authors of this paper and also editors of this book, felt we would like to make after having been involved in the editing and production of the book:

- Write sentences that contain comfortably one idea rather than two or more, without becoming too long and wordy.
- Aim for clarity. Simple is often better and is preferable to the complicated wordy language that people erroneously attribute to academic writing. Plain English is good English.
- The use of 'one' and 'we' is now obsolete in Academic English. The use of 'I' (first person singular) is acceptable when the author actually describes a process/research where he/she was actively involved and produced measurable outcomes.
- Insert headings and subheadings to break up large amounts of text and improve the clarity of the piece.
- Use tables and other visual materials only if they put forward the argument. Superfluous visual materials will weaken rather than strengthen the argument and the writing.
- Read the paper out loud. Very often the ears will tell you what the eyes won't, because as authors of a text people are often very close to the writing and need some distance to look at the text from a new perspective.
- Run the paper by a friend. An objective outsider, even if he/she is not a specialist in the field, will often be able to pick up incongruities and inconsistencies in the text.

Conclusion

In our opinion, editing and publishing are skills that can be taught and acquired at industry level in a learning environment designed to be open, flexible and intrinsically linked to practice. The present book is the outcome of an undergraduate university course, yet it complies with all current requirements and parameters in the industry. Hereby we are offering our work to the reading public and wish to thank Dr Mickan and the authors for their trust, support and collegiality.

References

Flann E, Hill B 2004, *The Australian Editing Handbook,* Fully revised and updated 2nd edition, John Wiley and Sons Australia, Ltd.

Homer, D, Petrescu, I, & Brewer, N 2004, *Talk of the Town,* Lythrum Press, Adelaide.

Kane, T 1994, *The New Oxford Guide to Writing,* Oxford University Press, Melbourne.

Kress, G 1997, 'Visual and verbal modes of representation in electronically mediated communication: the potentials of new forms of text' in *Page to screen: taking literacy into the electronic era,* ed I Snyder, Allen & Unwin, St Leonards, NSW, pp. 53–79.

Mackenzie, J 2004, *The Editor's Companion,* Cambridge University Press, Port Melbourne, Victoria.

Orrmulum, www.orrmulum.com.

Petrescu I, Brewer N 2005, *Heart of the Matter: An Introduction to Eighteen South Australian Poets,* Lythrum Press, Adelaide.

Petrescu I, Kilgariff K 2005, *The house that words built,* Lythrum Press, Adelaide, 2005.

Reep, DC 1997, *Technical writing: Principles, strategies and readings,* 3rd edn., Allyn and Bacon, Boston.

Spender L 2004, *Between the Lines: A Legal Guide for Writers and Illustrators,* Australian Society of Authors, Keesing Press, Strawberry Hills, NSW.

Stephens, M, Petrescu, I, Reu, A 2005, *Fuse or fracture: English as a world lingua franca,* UNISA, Adelaide.

Style manual for authors editors and printers, 2002, 6th edition, John Wiley and Sons Australia, Ltd.

Glossary and abbreviations

Abductive reasoning	Process of observing the facts and determining which theory/hypothesis applies to them, rather than beginning research with preconceptions
Allegory	Tale or story designed to highlight an important underlying point
A priori	Knowledge existing before experience
Authentic Texts	Texts written by L1 speakers
CALL	Computer Assisted Language Learning
Candidature	State of being a candidate (for higher education), preparation for same
CELTA	Certificate of English Language Teaching to Adults
CLT	Communicative Language Teaching
CSAT	College Scholastic Aptitude Test
Coalesce	Become whole
ConcApp	Concordancing program
Concordancing	Creating an index, categorising words or phrases
Conflate	Combine or integrate
Dong-A Daily	Daily newspaper in Korea
Dyadic	Two individuals or units considered a pair
Ecophysiological	Environmental physiology
EFL	English as a Foreign Language
ELL	English Language Learner
ESL	English as a Second Language
Extensive Reading	School-run program where EFL students are encouraged to read fiction for pleasure to aid language acquisition
Fragmentary	Fragmented. Consisting of many parts or fragments

Hierarchically	Where persons or things are placed in a graded order
IBP	Integrated Bridging Program
Intermittent	Occurring at different times; not continuous
IRE	Initiation, Response, Evaluation
IRF	Initiation, Response, Follow-up
Kibbitzing	Process of learning through watching an experienced person perform the activity to be learned
L1	First language
L2	Second language
Lexical	Relating to words or vocabulary
PDF	Portable Data File
Pedagogic	Pertaining to instruction or teaching
PEP	Pre-Enrolment Program
Phenomenological	Of the philosophical viewpoint of phenomenology; taking the essential meaning or essence from experience
Phonetic	Of or relating to speech sounds and their production
Pragmatic	Concerned with practical consequences or values
Praxis	Practice, as distinguished from theory
Qualitative	(Of research) Concerned with interpreting a subjective study rather than objective or quantitative experiments
Semiotics	The study of signs
SLA	Second Language Acquisition
Social semiotics	The study of signs in social situations specific to a community or culture
Solidarity	Union or fellowship arising from common responsibilities and interests
Synchronicity	Of occurring or 'being' simultaneously

Syntactical	Relating to the patterns of formation of sentences and phrases from words in a particular language
Sustained Silent Reading	An extended period of class time devoted to reading in silence
TOEIC	Test of English for International Communication
TOEFL	Test of English as a Foreign Language

References

Adams, R 2006, Factors affecting student use of concordancing: comparisons of instructional methodology, MA thesis, Centre for European Studies and General Linguistics, University of Adelaide, Adelaide.

Adult Migrant English Program 1992, *Certificate III in Spoken and Written English*, 4th edn, Department of Education and Training, Sydney.

Allwright, D & Bailey, KM 1991, *Focus on the language classroom: an introduction to classroom research for language teachers*, Cambridge University Press, New York.

Anton, M 1999, 'The discourse of a learner-centered classroom: sociocultural perspectives on teacher-learner interaction in the second-language classroom' in *The Modern Language Journal*, vol. 83, no. 3, pp. 303–318.

Arirang 2001, *News broadcast at 6:00 o'clock*, Arirang TV, Seoul.

Better choices, better health: summary report of the South Australian Generational Health Review 2003, South Australian Department of Human Services, Adelaide.

Blackledge, A & Pavlenko, A 2001, 'Negotiation of identities in multilingual contexts' in *The International Journal of Bilingualism*, vol. 5, no. 3, pp. 243–257.

Block, D 2003, *The social turn in second language acquisition*, Edinburgh University Press, Edinburgh.

Butt, D, Fahey, R, Feez, S, Spinks, S & Yallop, C 2003, *Using Functional Grammar: An Explorer's Guide*, National Centre for English Language Teaching and Research, Macquarie University, Sydney.

Cargill, M & Adams, R 2005, 'Learning discipline-specific research English for a world stage: a self-access concordancing tool' in *Higher Education in a Changing World: 2005 HERDSA Annual Conference*, Higher Education Research and Development Society of Australia, Sydney.

Cargill, M, Cadman, K & McGowan, U 2001, 'Postgraduate writing: using intersecting genres in a collaborative content-based program' in *Case Studies in TESOL: Academic Writing Programs*. ed I Leki, USA: Teaching English to Speakers of Other Languages (TESOL), Alexandria, pp. 85–96.

Cargill, M 1996, 'An integrated bridging program for international postgraduate students' in *Higher Education Research and Development*, vol. 15, no. 2, pp. 177–188.

Cass, A, Lowell, A, Christie, M, Snelling, PL, Flack, M, Marrnganyin, B, & Brown I 2002, 'Sharing the true stories: improving communication between Aboriginal patients and healthcare workers' in *Medical Journal of Australia*, vol. 176, pp. 466–470.

Cazden, CB 1988, *Classroom discourse: the language of teaching and learning*, Heinemann, Portsmouth.

Chen, T 2003, 'Reticence in class and on-line: two ESL students' experiences with communicative language teaching' in *System*, vol. 31, no. 2, pp. 259–281.

Cheng, X 2000, 'Asian students' reticence revisited' in *System*, vol. 28, no. 3, pp. 435–446.

Cho, Y 1998, 'A review on the recent trends of classroom instruction research in Korea' in *Education Anthropology Research*, vol. 1, no. 1, pp. 73–111.

Chowdhury, R 2003, 'International TESOL training and EFL contexts: The cultural disillusionment factor' in *Australian Journal of Education*, vol. 47, no. 3, pp. 283–302.

Christie, F 2002, *Classroom discourse analysis*, Continuum, New York.

Cobb, T 1997, 'Is there any measurable learning from hands-on concordancing?' in *System*, vol. 25, no. 3, pp. 301–315.

Console, D 2000, 'Teachers' action and student oral participation in classroom in *Second and foreign language learning through classroom interaction*, eds. JK Hall & LS Verplaetse, Lawrence Erlbaum, Mahwah, NJ, pp. 91–108.

Cortazzi, M & Jin, L 1999, 'Cultural mirrors: materials and methods in the EFL classroom' in *Culture in second language teaching and learning*, ed E Hinkel, Cambridge University Press, Cambridge, pp. 196–219.

Craswell, G 1992, 'International Graduate Coursework Students and the Urgency of Adapting to New Learning Strategies' Technical Report/Occasional Paper no. GS92/2, Graduate School, Australian National University, Canberra.

Dawson, R 1987, *The Present State of Australia*, Archival Facsimiles Limited, Alburgh.

De Guerrero, M & Villamil, O 2000, 'Activating the ZPD: Mutual Scaffolding in L2 Peer Revision' in *The Modern Language Journal*, vol. 84, no. 1, pp. 51–68.

Devitt, J & McMasters, A (eds) 1998a *Living on Medicine: a Cultural Study of End-stage Renal Disease among Aboriginal People*, I.A.D. Press, Alice Springs.

Devitt, J & McMasters, A (eds.) 1998b *On the Machine: Aboriginal Stories about Kidney Troubles*, I.A.D. Press, Alice Springs.

Dickinson, L 1994, *Self-instruction in language learning*, Cambridge University Press, Cambridge.

Dinsmore, D 1985, 'Waiting for Godot in the EFL classroom' in *ELT Journal*, vol. 39, no. 4, pp. 225–234.

Donato, R 2000, 'Sociocultural contributions to understanding the foreign and second language classroom' in *Sociocultural Theory and Second Language Learning*, ed JP Lantolf, Oxford University Press, Oxford & New York, pp. 27–50.

Duff, PA 2002, 'The Discursive Co-Construction of Knowledge, Identity and Difference: An Ethnography of Communication in the High School Mainstream' in *Applied Linguistics*, vol. 23, no. 3, pp. 289–322.

Dwyer, E & Heller MA 1996, 'Japanese Learners in Speaking Classes' in *Edinburgh Working Papers in Applied Linguistics,* no. 7, pp. 46–55.

Eades, D 1982, 'You Gotta Know How to Talk ... information seeking in South-East Queensland Aboriginal society' in *Australian Journal of Linguistics,* vol. 2, pp. 61–82.

Fairclough, N 1989, *Language and Power,* Longman, London & New York.

Farrell, TSC 2004, *Reflective practice in action: 80 reflection breaks for busy teachers,* Corwin Press, California.

Feez, S 2002, *Text-based Syllabus Design,* Adult Multicultural Education Service, Sydney.

Fenwick, C & Stevens, J 2004, 'Post Operative Pain Experiences of Central Australian Women: What Do We Understand?' in *Australian Journal of Rural Health,* vol. 12, pp. 22–27.

Firth, A & Wagner, J 1997, 'On discourse, communication, and (some) fundamental concepts in SLA research' in *The Modern Language Journal,* vol. 81, no. 3, pp. 285–300.

Flann, E, & Hill B 2004, *The Australian Editing Handbook,* Fully revised and updated 2nd edition, John Wiley and Sons Australia, Ltd.

Flood, RL 1999, *Rethinking the Fifth Discipline: Learning within the Unknowable,* Routledge, London.

Fox, M 2001, *Reading Magic,* Pan Macmillan Australia Pty Ltd, Melbourne.

Galbraith, B, Van Tassell, MA & Wells, G 1999, 'On Learning With and From Our Students' in *Dialogic Inquiry: Toward a Sociocultural Practice and Theory of Education,* Cambridge University Press, Cambridge, pp. 293–312.

Gee, JP & Green, J 1998, 'Discourse analysis, learning, and social practice: a methodological study' in *Review of Research in Education,* vol. 23, pp. 119–169.

Gledhill, C 1999b, 'The phraseology of rhetoric, collocations and discourse in cancer research abstracts' in *'Knowledge and Discourse'* International Multidisciplinary Conference, University of Hong Kong, Hong Kong.

Greaves, C. 1996, *ConcApp* Hong Kong: Edict Virtual Language Centre.

Gumperz, JJ 1982, *Discourse strategies,* Cambridge University Press, Cambridge.

Hall, ET 1966, *The Hidden Dimension,* Doubleday, New York.

Hall, ET 1959, *The Silent Language,* Doubleday, New York.

Hall, JK & Walsh, M 2002, 'Teacher-Student Interaction and Language Learning' in *Annual Review of Applied Linguistics,* vol. 22, pp. 186–203.

Hall, JK 1997, 'Differential teacher attention to student utterances: the construction of different opportunities for learning in the IRF' in *Linguistics and Education,* vol. 9, no. 3, pp. 287–311.

Hall, JK 1995, '(Re)creating our worlds with words: a sociohistorical perspective of face-to-face interaction' in *Applied Linguistics,* vol. 16, no. 2, pp. 206–232.

Hall, JK 1993, 'The role of oral practices in the accomplishment of our everyday lives: The sociocultural dimension of interaction with implications for the learning of another language' in *Applied Linguistics*, vol. 14, no. 2, pp. 145–166.

Halliday, MAK 1985, *An introduction to functional grammar*, Edward Arnold, London.

Halliday, MAK 1978, *Language as social semiotic: the social interpretation of language and meaning*, Edward Arnold, London.

Harkins, J 1994, *Bridging Two Worlds: Aboriginal English and Cross-cultural Understanding*, University of Queensland Press, St Lucia.

Harklau, L 1999, 'Representing Culture in the ESL Writing Classroom' in *Culture in Second Language Teaching and Learning*, ed E Hinkel, Cambridge University Press, Cambridge, pp. 109–130.

Harris, R 1998, Introduction *to Integrational Linguistics*, Pergamon, Oxford.

Harris, R 1996, *Signs, language and communication: integrational and segregational approaches*, Routledge, London.

Harris, R 1981, *The language myth*, Duckworth, London.

Hasan, R. & Williams, G (eds) 1996, *Literacy in society*, Longman, London.

Hassell, E 1975, *My Dusky Friends: Aboriginal life, customs and legends and glimpses of station life at Jarramungup in the 1880s*, CW Hassell, East Fremantle.

Heap, J 1985, 'Discourse in the production of classroom knowledge' in *Curriculum Inquiry*, vol. 15, no. 3, pp. 245–279.

Heath, SB 1983, *Ways with words: language, life and work in communities and classrooms*, Cambridge University Press, Cambridge.

Heritage, J 2001, 'Goffman, Garfinkel and Conversation Analysis' in *Discourse Theory and Practice*, eds. M Wetherall, S Taylor & SJ Yates, Sage Publications, Newbury Park, pp. 47–56.

Hicks, D 1996, 'Contextual inquiries: a discourse-oriented study of classroom learning' in *Discourse, learning, and schooling*, ed D Hicks, Cambridge University Press, Cambridge, pp. 104–141.

Hodge, R. and G. Kress 1988, *Social semiotics*, Polity Press, Oxford.

Homer D, Petrescu I, Brewer N 2004, *Talk of the Town*, Lythrum Press, Adelaide.

Jackson, J 2001, 'Reticence in second language case discussions: anxiety and aspirations' in *System*, vol. 30, no. 1, pp. 65–84.

Johns, T 1994, 'From printout to handout: grammar and vocabulary teaching in the context of data-driven learning' in *Approaches to Pedagogic Grammar*, ed T Odlin, Cambridge University Press, Cambridge, pp. 93–313.

Johns, T 1991, 'Should you be persuaded - two samples of data-driven learning materials' in *English Language Research Journal*, vol. 4, pp. 1–16.

Johns, T 1986, 'Micro-concord: a language-learner's research tool' in *System*, vol. 14, no. 2, pp. 151–162.

Johnson, KE 1995, *Understanding communication in second language classroom*, Cambridge University Press, New York.

Jones, JF 1999, 'From Silence to Talk: Cross Cultural Ideas on Students' Participation in Academic Group Discussion' in *English for Specific Purposes*, vol. 18, no. 3, pp. 243–259.

Kane, T 1994, *The New Oxford Guide to Writing*, Oxford University Press, Melbourne.

Kong, A & Pearson, PD 2003, 'The road to participation: the construction of a literacy practice in a learning community of linguistically diverse learners' in *Research in the Teaching of English*, vol. 38, no. 1, pp. 85–124.

Koole, T 2003, 'The Interactive Construction of Heterogeneity in the Classroom' in *Linguistics and Education*, vol. 14, no. 1, pp. 3–26.

Koyama, Y, Nakano T and Matsuura C 2003, 'Development of an ESP E-Learning Tool Using In-House Corpora' in *Knowledge-based Information and Engineering Systems, 7th International Conference*, KES 2003, pp. 533–539, Springer, Oxford.

Kramsch, C. (ed) 2002, *Language acquisition and language socialisation*, Continuum, London.

Krashen, S 1993, *The power of reading*, Libraries Unlimited Inc, Englewood, Colorado.

Kress, G 1997, 'Visual and verbal modes of representation in electronically mediated communication: the potentials of new forms of text' in *Page to screen: taking literacy into the electronic era*, ed I Snyder, Allen & Unwin, St Leonards, NSW, pp. 53–79.

Lave, J & Wenger, E 1991, *Situated Learning: Legitimate Peripheral Participation*, Cambridge University Press, Cambridge.

Lee, D & Swales, J 2006, 'A corpus-based EAP course for NNS doctoral students: Moving from available specialized corpora to self-compiled corpora'in *English for Specific Purposes*, vol. 25, pp. 56–75.

Lemke, JL 1990, *Talking Science: Language, Learning, and Values*, NJ: Ablex, Norwood.

Lemke, JL 2003, 'Identity, Development, and Desire: Critical Questions' in *The AERA (American Educational Research Association (Conference)*, Chicago.

Lewis, M 1994, *The Lexical Approach*, Language Teaching Publications, London.

Lim, I-J 2003, 'Classroom observation of a Korean EFL teacher's strategies in a public elementary school context: a case study' in *Ohak Yonku/Language Research*, vol. 39, no. 3, pp. 663–693.

Lin, A 1999a 'Doing-English-lessons in the reproduction or transformation of social worlds?' in *TESOL Quarterly*, vol. 33, no. 3, pp. 393–412.

Lin, A 1999b 'Resistance and creativity in English reading lessons in Hong Kong' in *Language, Culture and Curriculum*, vol. 12, no. 3, pp. 285–296.

Liu, NF & Littlewood W 1997, 'Why do many students appear reluctant to participate in classroom learning discourse' in *System*, vol. 25, no. 3, pp. 371–384.

Mackenzie, J 2004, *The Editor's Companion*, Cambridge University Press, Port Melbourne, Victoria.

Malcolm IG & Koscielecki, MM 1997, *Aboriginality and English: Report to the Australian Research Council*, Centre for Applied Language Research, Edith Cowan University, Mount Lawley.

Maynard, DW 1992, '"On Clinicians co-implicating recipients" perspective in the delivery of diagnostic news' in *Talk at Work: Interaction in Institutional settings*, eds. P Drew & J Heritage, Cambridge University Press, Cambridge, pp. 331–358.

McCarthy, M & Carter, R 1994, 'Designing the discourse syllabus' in *Language as Discourse Perspectives for Language Teaching*, Longman Group Limited, London.

Mehan, H 1979, *Learning lessons: social organization in the classroom*, Harvard University Press, Cambridge & Massachusetts.

Mickan, P 2003, 'Beyond grammar: text as unit of analysis' in *Grammar in the Language Classroom: Changing Approaches and Practices*' ed J. James, Singapore, SEAMEO Regional Language Centre, pp. 220–227.

Mickan, P (in press) 'Doing science and home economics: curriculum socialisation of new arrivals to Australia' in *Language and Education: An International Journal*.

Mickan, P 2006, 'Socialisation through teacher talk in an Australian bilingual class' in *International Journal of Bilingual Education and Bilingualism*, vol 9, no.3, pp. 342–358.

Mickan, P 2004, 'Teaching methodologies' in *Teaching English in Australia: theoretical perspectives and practical issues*, ed C Conlon, API Network, Australia Research Institute, Perth: WA, pp. 171–191.

Miller, J 1999, 'Becoming Audible: social identity and second language use' in *Journal of Intercultural Studies*, vol. 20, no. 2, pp. 149–165.

Millett, E 1980, *An Australian Parsonage or the Settler and the Savage in Western Australia*, University of Western Australia Press, Nedlands.

Ministry of Education 1997, *Foreign Language Education Curriculum*, Ministry of Education, Seoul.

Mithen, S 1996, *The Prehistory Of The Mind: A Search For The Origin Of Art, Religion and Science*, Phoenix Paperbacks, Orion Books Ltd, London.

Nelson, M. 2003, 'Worldly Experience' in *Guardian Weekly*, 20 March, 2003.

Nystrand, M 1997a 'Dialogic instruction: when recitation becomes conversation' in *Opening dialogue: understanding the dynamics of language learning and teaching in the English classroom*, Teachers College Press, New York.

Ochs, E 1988, *Culture and language development: language acquisition and language socialisation in a Samoan village,* Cambridge University Press, Cambridge.

Ochs, E, & Schieffelin, BB 1984, 'Language acquisition and socialization: three developmental stories and their implications' in *Culture theory: essays on mind, self and emotion,* eds. RA Shweder & RA LeVine, Cambridge University Press, New York.

Olson, DR 1991, 'Children's understanding of interpretation and the autonomy of written texts' in *Text,* vol. 11, no. 1, pp. 3–23.

Ong, LML, DeHaes, JCJM, Hoos, AM & Lammes FB 1995, 'Doctor-Patient Communication: A Review of the Literature' in *Social Science and Medicine,* vol. 40, no. 7, pp. 903–918.

Painter, C 1989, 'Learning language: a functional view of language development' in *Language development: learning language, learning culture,* eds. R Hasan & JR Martin, Ablex, Norwood, NJ, vol. 27, pp. 18–65.

Petrescu I, Brewer, N 2005, *Heart of the Matter: An Introduction to Eighteen South Australian Poets,* Lythrum Press, Adelaide.

Petrescu I, Kilgariff, K 2005, *The house that words built,* Lythrum Press, Adelaide.

Reep, DC 1997, *Technical writing: Principles, strategies and readings,* 3rd edn., Allyn and Bacon, Boston.

Rogoff, B 1990, *Apprenticeship in thinking: cognitive development in social context,* Oxford University Press, New York.

Rommetveit, R 1983, 'In search of a truly interdisciplinary semantics. A sermon on hopes of salvation from hereditary sins' in *Journal of Semantics,* vol. 2, pp. 1–28.

Sanderson, P 1999, *Using newspapers in the classroom,* Cambridge University Press, Cambridge.

Sawir, E 2005, 'Language difficulties of international students in Australia: The effects of prior learning experience' in *International Education Journal,* vol.6, no. 5, pp. 567–580..

Scheflen, AE 1972, *Body Language and the Social Order,* Prentice Hall, Englewood Cliffs.

Schieffelin, BB & Ochs, E 1986, 'Language Socialization' in *Annual Review of Anthropology,* vol. 15, pp. 163–191.

Scovel, T 1994, 'The Role of Culture in Second Language Pedagogy' in *System,* vol. 22, no. 2, pp. 205–219.

Sit, MK 2003, Singlish – threat and threatened, BA Hons thesis, University of Adelaide.

Soars, L & Soars, J 2003, *New Headway Intermediate,* Oxford University Press, Oxford.

Spender L 2004, *Between the Lines: A Legal Guide for Writers and Illustrators,* Australian Society of Authors, Keesing Press, Strawberry Hills, NSW.

Stephens, M, Petrescu, I, Reu, A 2005, *Fuse or fracture: English as a world lingua franca*, UNISA, Adelaide.

Stevens, V 1995, 'Concordancing with Language Learners: Why? When? What?' in *CAELL Journal*, vol. 6, no. 2, pp. 2–10.

Storch, N 2002, 'Patterns of Interaction in ESL Pair Work' in *Language Learning*, vol. 52, no. 1, pp. 119–158.

Style manual for authors editors and printers, 2002, 6th edition, John Wiley and Sons Australia, Ltd.

Swain, M, Brooks, L & Tocalli-Beller, A 2002, 'Peer-peer dialogue as a means of second language learning' in *Annual Review of Applied Linguistics*, vol. 22, pp. 171–185.

Swain, M & Lapkin, S 1998, 'Interaction and Second Language Learning: Two Adolescent French Immersion Students Working Together' in *The Modern Language Journal*, vol. 82, no. 3, pp. 320–337.

Swales, JM.& Feak, C 2000. *English in today's research world: a writing guide*, University of Michigan Press, Ann Arbor.

Swann, J 1994, 'Observation and Recording Talk in Educational Settings' in *Researching Language and Literacy in Social Context*, eds. D Graddol, J Maybin, & B Stierer, Multilingual Matters, Clevedon, pp. 26–48.

Sykes, JB (ed) 1989, *The Concise Oxford Dictionary*, Oxford University Press, Oxford.

Teramoto, H. and Mickan P (in press), Writing a critical review: reflections on literacy practices' in *Language Awareness*.

Thurstun, J & Candlin, C 1998, 'Concordancing and the teaching of the vocabulary of academic English' in *English for Specific Purposes*, vol.17, no.3, pp. 267–280.

Thurstun, J & Candlin, CN 1993, *Exploring Academic English: A workbook for student essay writing*, NCELTR, Macquarie University, Sydney.

Todd, RW 2001, 'Induction from self-selected concordances and self-correction' in *System*, vol.29, no. 1, pp. 91–102.

Toohey, K 1996, 'Learning English as a second language in kindergarten: a community of practice perspective' in *Canadian Modern Language Review*, vol. 52, no. 4, p. 553.

Toohey, K 2000, *Learning English at school: identity, social relations and classroom practice*, Multilingual Matters, Clevedon.

Tribble, C & Jones, G 1997, *Concordances in the Classroom*, Athelstan, Houston.

Tribble, C 1989, 'The use of text structuring vocabulary in native and non-native speaker writing' in *MUESLI News*, June, pp. 17–20.

Troy, J 1990, 'Australian Aboriginal Contact with the English language in New South Wales: 1788-1845', monograph in *Pacific Linguistics*, Series B, pp. 103.

Trudgen, R 2000, *Why Warriors Lie Down and Die*, Aboriginal Resource and Development Services, Darwin.

Tsui, ABM 1991, 'Learner Involvement and Comprehensible Input' in *RELC Journal*, vol. 22, no. 2, pp. 44–60.

Unsworth, L 2000, *Researching language in schools and communities: functional linguistic perspectives*, Cassell, London.

Van Leeuwen, T 2005, *Introducing social semiotics*, London, Routledge.

Volosinov, VN 1973, *Marxism and the philosophy of language*, translated by Ladislav Matejka and I. R. Titunik, Seminar Press, New York.

von Hugel, BC 1994, *New Holland Journal: November 1833 – October 1834*, translated by Dymphna Clark., Melbourne University Press, Melbourne.

Vygotsky, LS 1987, *Thinking and speech*, Plenum, New York.

Vygotsky, LS 1978, *Mind in Society*, Harvard University Press, Cambridge & Massachusetts.

Walkerdine, V 1982, 'From context to text: a psychosemiotic approach to abstract thought' in *Children thinking through language*, eds. M Beveridge & E Arnold, London.

Warschauer, M 1996, 'Computer-assisted language learning: An introduction' in *Multimedia language teaching*, ed S Fotos, Logos International, Tokyo, pp. 3–20.

Watson, M 1987, 'The communication problems of tribal Aboriginal women in the maternity ward' in *Darwin Education Studies Department*, Darwin Institute of Technology, Darwin.

Weeramanthri, T 1997, '"Painting a Leonardo with Finger Paint": Medical Practitioners Communicating about Death with Aboriginal People' in *Social Science and Medicine*, vol. 45, no. 7, pp. 1005–1015.

Wells, G 1999, *Dialogic inquiry: towards a sociocultural practice and theory of education* Cambridge University Press, Cambridge.

Wells, G & Chang-Wells, GL 1992, *Constructing knowledge together: classrooms as centers of inquiry and literacy*, Heinemann, Portsmouth.

Wells, G and Claxton, G 2002, *Learning for life in the 21st century: sociocultural perspectives on the future of education*, Blackwell, Oxford.

Wenger, E 1998, *Communities of Practice: Learning, Meaning and Identity*, Cambridge University Press, Cambridge.

Wertsch, J 1991, *Voices of the mind: a sociocultural approach to mediated action*, Cambridge University Press, Cambridge & Massachusetts.

Yalden, J 1987, 'Discourse analysis and course design' in *Principles of Course Design for Language Teaching*, Cambridge University Press, Cambridge.

Websites

Amer, A 2003, 'Teaching EFL/ESL Literature' in *The Reading Matrix*, vol. 3, no. 2, viewed 8 August 2003, <http://www.readingmatrix.com/articles/amer/article.pdf>

Asraf, RM & Ahmad, IS 2003, 'Promoting English language development and the reading habit among students in rural schools through the Guided Extensive Reading program' in *Reading in a Foreign Language*, vol. 15, no. 2, http://nflrc.hawaii.edu/rfl/October2003/mohdasraf/mohdasraf.html

Day, R and Bamford, J 2000, 'Reaching Reluctant Readers' in *Forum ENGLISH TEACHING*, vol. 38 no. 3, <http://exchanges.state.gov/forum/vols/vol38/no3/p12.htm>

Day, R and Bamford, J 2002, 'Top Ten Principles for Teaching Extensive Reading' in *Reading in a Foreign Language*, vol. 14, no. 2, viewed 17 August 2003 <http://nflrc.hawaii.edu/rfl/October2002/day/day.html>

Edis, F 1998, 'Just Scratching the Surface: Miscommunication in Aboriginal Health Care' in *Masters Report*, viewed 17 August 2004, <http://www.sharingtruestories.com>

Elley, W 1996, 'Lifting Literacy Levels with Story Books: Evidence from the South Pacific, Singapore, Sri Lanka and South Africa', International Literacy Institute, viewed 21 June 2003, <http://www.literacyonline.org/products/ili/pdf/ilprocwe.pdf>

www.enchantedlearning.com 2004, *Vocabulary Map Graphic Organizers*, viewed 11 June 2004 <http://www.enchantedlearning.com/graphicorganizers/vocab/index.html>

Gledhill, C 2000, 'The discourse function of collocation in research article introductions' in *English for Specific Purposes*, vol. 19, pp. 115-135, viewed 17 August 2003, <www.elsevier.com/locate/esp>

Hwang. SK 2001, 'Reading Skill Development of an ESL Student: A Four-Year Longitudinal Study' in *Korea TESOL Journal*, vol. 4, viewed 8 August, <http://www.kotesol.org/pubs/journal/2001/abs_sang.shtml>

Lee, D 2001, 'Genres, Registers, Text Types, Domains and Styles: Clarifying the Concepts and Navigating a Path Through the BNC Jungle' in. *Language Learning and Technology*, vol. 5, no.3, pp. 37-72, viewed 24 March 2006 <http://llt.msu.edu/vol5num3/lee/default.html >

Levin-Rozalis, M 2004, 'Searching For The Unknowable: A Process Of Detection— Abductive Research Generated By Projective Techniques' in *International Journal of Qualitative Methods*, vol 3, iss 2, viewed 10 June 2005, <http://www.ualberta.ca/~iiqm/backissues/3_2/pdf/rozalis.pdf>

Nation, P 1997, *The Language Learning Benefits of Extensive Reading*, <http://www.jalt-publications.org/tlt/files/97/may/benefits.html>

Neyman, PF 2002, 'Helping Children Learn to Think in English Through Reading Storybooks' in *The Internet TESL Journal*, vol. 8, no. 8, viewed 2 October 2003, <http://iteslj.org/Articles/Neyman-Storybooks/>

Orrmulum, <www.orrmulum.com>

Paterson, B, Bottorff, J, & Hewatt, R 2003, 'Blending Observational Methods: Possibilities, Strategies, And Challenges' in *International Journal of Qualitative Methods*, vol 2, iss 1, viewed 11 June 2005, <http://www.ualberta.ca/~iiqm/backissues/2_1/ html/patersonetal.html>

Shank, G 1995, 'Semiotics And Qualitative Research In Education: The Third Crossroad' in *The Qualitative Report*, vol 2, iss 3, viewed 8 June 2005, <http://www.nova.edu/ssss/QR/QR2-3/shank.html>

Waring, R 2004, 'What is extensive reading?', viewed 12 May 2004, <http://wwwl.harenet.ne.jp/~waring/er/er_faq.htm>

Contributors

Peter Mickan is Head of the Discipline of Linguistics at the University of Adelaide, Adelaide 5005, South Australia. Email address for correspondence peter.mickan@adelaide.edu.au

Ioana Petrescu, a Senior Lecturer in Professional and Creative Writing at the University of South Australia, is the author of two books, editor of five books, and has been widely published as an academic and creative writer. Her latest publication as editor is *The house that words built* (Lythrum Press, Adelaide, 2005).

Ray Adams has completed the MA Applied Linguistics in the Discipline of Linguistics at the University of Adelaide and is a Lecturer and Academic Skills Advisor in the Student Learning Centre at Flinders University, South Australia.

Simon Eddy is a postgraduate student in Applied Linguistics in the Discipline of Linguistics at the University of Adelaide.

Glenda Inverarity is a PhD student in the Discipline of Linguistics at the University of Adelaide and a Lecturer in English Language Services in TAFE.

Dongjin Kim graduated with MA Applied Linguistics from the Discipline of Linguistics at the University of Adelaide and now teaches English in Korea

Mi-ok Lim is a PhD student in the Discipline of Linguistics at the University of Adelaide.

Johanna Motteram is an MA Applied Linguistics student in the Discipline of Linguistics at the University of Adelaide.

Fiona Ryan graduated with MA Applied Linguistics from the Discipline of Linguistics at the University of Adelaide and is a Research Associate in the Faculty of Health Sciences at Flinders University, South Australia.

Judith Timoney is a student in the Bachelor of Arts program at the University of South Australia, majoring in Professional and Creative Communication.

Lythrum Press

ADELAIDE

www.lythrumpress.com.au